WOMEN EMPOWERMENT AND INCLUSIVE GROWTH

EMPOWERING WOMEN. ENABLING PROGRESS.

AN EDITED BOOK

To the women who lead with courage,
To the voices long unheard but never silenced,
To the changemakers in every corner of the world—
breaking barriers, uplifting communities, and inspiring generations.

This book is dedicated to all who believe in the power of equity,
the strength of inclusion,
and the promise of a future where every woman thrives.

Contents

Contents

Foreword

In the 21st century, the discourse on development, equity, and sustainability is incomplete without the central inclusion of gender justice and women's empowerment. Across the globe, women continue to play vital roles in shaping economies, leading communities, innovating technologies, and preserving cultures. Yet, they remain underrepresented in decision-making processes and overburdened by systemic inequalities.

Women Empowerment and Inclusive Growth: Empowering Women and Enabling Progress is both a timely and necessary contribution to the global conversation on inclusive development. This edited volume brings together diverse voices, perspectives, and disciplines to examine the multifaceted dimensions of women's empowerment—from economic participation and political representation to digital inclusion, legal frameworks, and environmental leadership.

Each chapter offers a critical yet hopeful lens, presenting both challenges and pathways forward. Grounded in empirical insights, case studies, and policy analysis, the book underscores a powerful truth: when women thrive, societies prosper. Empowerment is not a zero-sum goal; it is a collective imperative that enhances resilience, equity, and human dignity for all.

This volume is not just a scholarly endeavor but a call to action—for educators, policymakers, entrepreneurs, activists, and students alike. It challenges us to rethink traditional paradigms, to design systems that uplift rather than marginalize, and to commit to a future where inclusion is not optional but essential.

May this book inspire reflection, dialogue, and most importantly, transformation.

Preface

The pursuit of inclusive growth cannot be achieved without recognizing and addressing the systemic inequalities that women face across social, economic, political, and cultural domains. This book, Women Empowerment and Inclusive Growth: Empowering Women and Enabling Progress, emerges from a commitment to center women's experiences, voices, and leadership in the broader narrative of development and equity.

The idea for this volume was born out of a recognition that while there is growing global awareness of gender disparities, there is still a pressing need to translate that awareness into inclusive policies, equitable practices, and transformative action. Empowering women is not just a goal—it is a foundation for sustainable development, democratic governance, and social justice.

This edited collection brings together scholars, practitioners, and thought leaders who explore the diverse dimensions of women's empowerment—ranging from economic participation and political representation to technological inclusion, health equity, environmental leadership, and innovation. Each chapter examines both the progress made and the gaps that remain, offering case studies, critical analyses, and forward-looking strategies to guide future interventions.

The contributors come from varied disciplinary backgrounds and geographic contexts, reflecting the intersectional and global nature of the issues addressed. Together, their insights provide a comprehensive understanding of how gender equality can be achieved through collaborative, inclusive, and multidimensional approaches.

It is our hope that this book serves not only as an academic resource but also as a catalyst for dialogue, policy reform, and grassroots action. Whether you are a student, educator, policymaker, activist, or development practitioner, may this volume inform, inspire, and empower you to contribute to a more just and inclusive world.

Acknowledgements

This book is the result of collective insight, tireless effort, and shared commitment to the ideals of gender equality and inclusive development. We extend our heartfelt gratitude to all the contributors whose chapters form the core of this volume. Their rigorous research, critical perspectives, and passion for empowering women have enriched this work beyond measure.

We are deeply thankful to the scholars, practitioners, and thought leaders who reviewed the chapters and offered invaluable feedback. Their academic generosity and constructive guidance helped strengthen the quality and relevance of the content.

Special thanks go to our institutional partners and academic collaborators, whose support—logistical, intellectual, and moral—was vital throughout the development of this book. We also acknowledge the editorial and publishing teams for their professionalism, patience, and dedication in bringing this project to completion.

Special thanks are due to Dr. Durgesh Singh, Assistant Consultant at Tata Consultancy Services. His insightful guidance, timely encouragement, and technical input played a vital role in making this volume possible. His support was instrumental throughout the editorial process.

We are especially grateful to the countless women across the world—activists, entrepreneurs, workers, caregivers, educators, and leaders—who continue to inspire change in the face of adversity. Their lived experiences, resilience, and vision are the true foundation of this book.

Finally, to our families, mentors, and colleagues who stood by us during the long hours of research, writing, and editing—your encouragement made this journey possible.

This book is for everyone who believes in a fairer, more inclusive, and more equitable world.

Prologue

Throughout history, the contributions of women have often been overlooked, undervalued, or written out of the dominant narratives of progress and development. Yet women have always been at the forefront of change—building communities, driving economies, shaping cultures, and advocating for justice. Today, in an era defined by rapid technological advancement, globalization, and complex societal challenges, the imperative to recognize, support, and amplify women's roles in shaping inclusive growth is more urgent than ever.

Women Empowerment and Inclusive Growth: Empowering Women and Enabling Progress is more than a collection of academic essays. It is a dialogue across disciplines, regions, and generations—a platform to explore what it truly means to empower women and how such empowerment can transform societies. The chapters in this volume reflect diverse perspectives, lived experiences, and intersecting realities, underscoring the idea that empowerment is not a one-size-fits-all concept. It is contextual, dynamic, and deeply rooted in local cultures, policies, histories, and aspirations.

This book does not merely document progress or analyze persistent challenges; it envisions a future. A future where women are not just participants in development but architects of it. A future where inclusive growth is not an aspiration but a shared reality.

As readers journey through the chapters, they will encounter stories of resilience and innovation, insights grounded in research, and strategies aimed at reshaping institutions and mindsets. May this book serve as both a mirror and a roadmap—reflecting the world as it is and guiding us toward the world as it should be.

Women Empowerment and Inclusive Growth: Conceptual Foundations

Author: Dr. Rakesh Verma, Assistant professor at Dr. Shakuntala Misra National Rehabilitation University, Lucknow

Abstract

This chapter establishes the conceptual groundwork for understanding the critical link between women's empowerment and inclusive growth. It begins by defining key concepts such as empowerment, gender equality, and inclusive development, and then reviews prominent theoretical frameworks that explain how empowering women contributes to social and economic progress. The chapter further examines global trends and development discourses that emphasize gender inclusion as essential for sustainable growth. Drawing on empirical studies and policy insights, it highlights how women's increased participation in education, labor markets, and decision-making processes can drive poverty reduction, enhance productivity, and promote equitable development. Ultimately, the chapter underscores that empowering women is not only a matter of social justice but a strategic imperative for achieving comprehensive and lasting inclusive growth.

1. Introduction

In recent decades, the discourse on development has undergone a transformative shift from a narrow focus on economic growth to a broader understanding of inclusive and equitable progress. Central to this shift is the recognition of gender equality and women empowerment as not only moral imperatives but also strategic priorities for nations seeking to ensure sustainability, equity, and resilience.

This chapter seeks to examine the foundational concepts of women empowerment and inclusive growth. It outlines how these concepts intersect, complement, and reinforce one another in the broader context of social transformation and sustainable development.

2. Defining Women Empowerment

Women empowerment is the process through which women acquire the capacity to make independent decisions and fully exercise their rights across all areas of life. It encompasses access to essential resources such as education, healthcare, and economic opportunities, as well as meaningful participation and representation in political, social, and economic institutions. Empowerment is both an ongoing process and a transformative goal, requiring the removal of structural barriers, cultural norms, and discriminatory practices that limit women's agency. Ultimately, it seeks to create an environment where women can realize their potential on equal footing with men, thereby fostering individual well-being and societal progress.

Key dimensions of women empowerment include:

Women empowerment spans several interconnected dimensions:

- **Economic empowerment:** Ensures women have access to income-generating opportunities, secure employment, land ownership, credit facilities, and the ability to start and manage businesses. Economic autonomy strengthens their financial independence and decision-making power.
- **Social empowerment:** Involves equal access to quality education, healthcare services, and active participation in community and social life. It fosters social inclusion and challenges traditional gender roles.
- **Political empowerment:** Focuses on women's engagement in governance, policymaking, and leadership positions at local, national, and global levels, enabling them to influence decisions that affect their lives and communities.
- **Psychological empowerment:** Builds women's self-esteem, confidence, and resilience, helping them overcome fear, coercion, and societal pressures to assert control over their own lives.

Key Dimensions of Women's Empowerment

What affects a women's ability to control her own circumstances and fulfil her own interests and priorities?

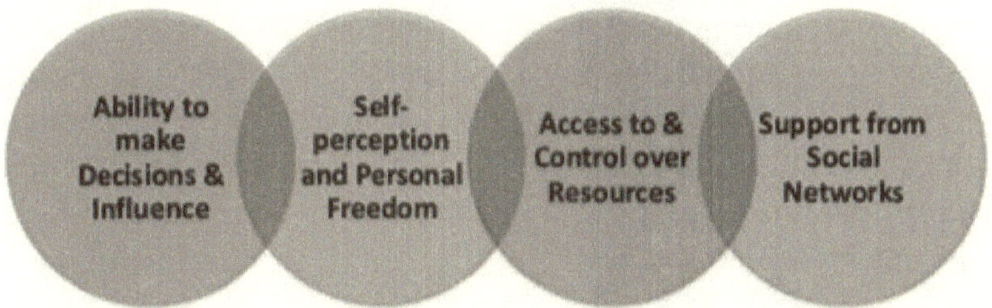

Key dimensions of women empowerment

Women's empowerment is multifaceted and must be contextualized within historical, cultural, and institutional realities.

3. Understanding Inclusive Growth

Inclusive growth is defined as economic growth that is sustained over time and shared equitably across society. Unlike traditional growth models that focus solely on GDP expansion, inclusive growth emphasizes broad-based participation and equitable distribution of benefits. It targets:

- **Equity in Opportunity:** Guaranteeing that everyone, regardless of gender or background, has fair access to fundamental services such as education, healthcare, and essential infrastructure. This levels the playing field and enables marginalized groups, especially women, to participate fully in economic and social life.

- **Social Protection:** Implementing measures to shield vulnerable populations from economic shocks, poverty, and social exclusion. Social safety nets, such as healthcare support, unemployment benefits, and targeted welfare programs, help reduce inequalities and promote resilience.

- **Institutional Reforms:** Strengthening governance through transparent, accountable, and inclusive institutions. Effective institutions ensure that policies and resources reach those most in need, uphold rights, and create an enabling environment for sustainable and equitable development.

Inclusive growth strives to reduce poverty, inequality, and marginalization, thus fostering cohesive and sustainable societies.

4. Conceptual Linkages Between Empowerment and Inclusive Growth

Women empowerment and inclusive growth are deeply interlinked. Empowering women enhances their productive capacities, facilitates participation in decision-making, and improves overall family and community wellbeing. Simultaneously, inclusive growth policies create the enabling environment necessary for empowerment to take root.

Key intersections include:

- **Labor Market Participation:** When empowered women join the workforce, they contribute to higher productivity, innovation, and economic growth. Their participation broadens the talent pool and drives more diverse and dynamic workplaces.
- **Education and Health:** Investing in women's education and health not only improves their well-being but also generates long-term benefits for families and communities. Educated and healthy women tend to raise healthier, better-educated children, creating positive intergenerational effects.
- **Entrepreneurship:** Women-led businesses play a crucial role in diversifying economies, creating jobs, and enhancing local resilience, especially in underserved communities. Supporting female entrepreneurship fuels inclusive economic development.
- **Leadership:** Increasing women's representation in political and organizational leadership fosters more inclusive decision-making processes. It ensures that policies and programs better reflect the needs of diverse populations, promoting equitable growth.

Empirical research consistently demonstrates that gender equality is associated with higher economic growth, lower poverty rates, and more responsive institutions.

5. Theoretical Perspectives

Understanding women empowerment and its relationship to inclusive growth requires engaging with several key theoretical frameworks:

5.1 Capabilities Approach

Developed by Amartya Sen and Martha Nussbaum, the Capabilities Approach centers on individuals' genuine ability to pursue lives they have reason to value. Rather than focusing solely on economic wealth or resources, this framework emphasizes expanding real freedoms and opportunities—known as "capabilities"—that allow women to make meaningful choices. In the context of women empowerment, it highlights the importance of removing social, cultural, and institutional barriers so that women can fully participate in all aspects of life, including education, health, political engagement, and economic activities. This approach shifts the focus from mere outcomes to enhancing women's actual freedoms to shape their own lives.

5.2 Feminist Economics

Feminist economics critiques traditional economic theories for overlooking the gendered nature of labor, especially the significant yet unpaid care work predominantly carried out by women. It challenges the narrow focus on market transactions by highlighting how unpaid household and caregiving activities contribute to overall economic well-being. This perspective calls for gender-responsive policies and budgeting that recognize and value women's economic contributions both inside and outside formal markets. By addressing structural inequalities and power imbalances, feminist economics seeks to create more inclusive economic systems that support women's empowerment and broader social justice.

5.3 Intersectionality

Coined by Kimberlé Crenshaw, intersectionality highlights how women's experiences of empowerment and marginalization are shaped by the overlapping and interconnected nature of social identities such as race, class, caste, ability, sexual orientation, and more. This framework reveals that gender cannot be understood in isolation, as women face multiple and compounded forms of discrimination and privilege. Consequently, effective empowerment strategies must recognize this diversity and complexity, tailoring interventions to address the specific needs of different groups to ensure genuine and inclusive empowerment for all women.

6. Global Trends and Policy Commitments

Internationally, there is growing consensus on the need to center women in development strategies:

- **Sustainable Development Goals (SDGs):** Particularly Goal 5, which focuses on achieving gender equality and empowering all women and girls, and Goal 8, which promotes sustained, inclusive economic growth and decent work for all. These goals emphasize women's central role in sustainable development.
- **Convention on the Elimination of All Forms of Discrimination Against Women (CEDAW):** An international treaty that obligates signatory states to take comprehensive measures to eliminate gender discrimination and promote women's rights across political, economic, social, and cultural domains.
- **Beijing Platform for Action (1995):** A landmark global agenda that outlines strategic objectives and actions to accelerate progress toward gender equality, emphasizing areas such as education, health, economic participation, and decision-making power.

Many countries have introduced gender budgeting, equal pay legislation, and inclusive social protection programs. However, implementation gaps, cultural resistance, and underfunding remain persistent obstacles.

7. Barriers to Women Empowerment and Inclusive Growth

Despite widespread acknowledgement of the importance of gender equity, significant barriers remain:

- **Structural Inequality:** Deep-rooted patriarchal institutions and entrenched social norms continue to restrict women's freedoms and limit their choices across social, economic, and political spheres.
- **Economic Disparities:** Women often experience wage gaps, occupational segregation into lower-paid or informal sectors, and face significant barriers in accessing financial services and credit.
- **Underrepresentation:** Despite progress, women remain significantly underrepresented in political leadership roles and corporate boardrooms, limiting their influence on key decisions and policies.
- **Digital Divide:** Women are less likely than men to have access to digital technologies and the internet, hindering their ability to engage in the growing knowledge economy and benefit from digital innovation.
- **Gender-Based Violence:** Violence against women remains a widespread and persistent threat, undermining their safety, dignity, and ability to participate fully in society.

These challenges are often magnified in rural, conflict-affected, or marginalized communities, necessitating intersectional and context-specific responses.

8. A Framework for Integration

A successful approach to linking women empowerment with inclusive growth must be:

- **Rights-based:** Rooted in legal and institutional commitments to gender equality, ensuring that empowerment efforts uphold women's fundamental human rights and promote justice.
- **Participatory:** Actively involving women's voices and perspectives at every stage of policy formulation, program design, and implementation to ensure relevance and responsiveness.
- **Transformative:** Focused on shifting power relations and dismantling the deep-seated structural inequalities that sustain gender discrimination and social exclusion.
- **Data-driven:** Guided by robust sex-disaggregated data and gender analysis to identify gaps, measure progress, and design targeted interventions.
- **Collaborative:** Engaging a broad range of stakeholders—including governments, civil society, the private sector, and international organizations—to foster coordinated and sustained action.

Such a framework ensures that empowerment is not symbolic but substantive, and that growth is not only inclusive in outcome but in process.

9. Conclusion

Women empowerment and inclusive growth are two sides of the same coin. Empowering women is essential for realizing the full potential of societies—socially, politically, and economically. Inclusive growth, in turn, is sustainable only when it actively addresses the needs, rights, and aspirations of women and girls.

This chapter has laid the conceptual groundwork for understanding this critical nexus. The chapters that follow will delve deeper into sector-specific analyses—ranging from education and digital transformation to governance and entrepreneurship—demonstrating how theory can inform transformative practice.

References

- *Sen, A. (1999). Development as Freedom. Oxford University Press.*
- *Nussbaum, M. (2000). Women and Human Development: The Capabilities Approach. Cambridge University Press.*
- *UN Women. (2023). Gender Equality: Realizing Rights for All.*
- *World Bank. (2023). Women, Business and the Law.*
- *Crenshaw, K. (1989). Demarginalizing the Intersection of Race and Sex.*
- *ILO. (2023). Global Wage Report.*
- *UNDP. (2022). Gender Equality Strategy.*
- *OECD. (2022). Measuring Inclusive Growth and Well-being.*

CHAPTER TWO

Gender Equality in Historical and Global Contexts

Author: Dr. Santosh Kumar Yadav, Research Scholar at Magadh University Bodhgaya Bihar

Abstract

This chapter examines the evolution of gender equality from historical and global perspectives. It traces the shifting roles, rights, and social status of women across diverse civilizations, highlighting how cultural, economic, and political forces have influenced gender relations over time. The chapter also reviews significant international milestones in the struggle for gender equality and compares progress and persistent disparities across different regions. By analyzing these dynamics, the chapter sheds light on the complex challenges and achievements on the path toward global gender parity.

1. Introduction

Gender equality—the state in which individuals of all genders have equal rights, responsibilities, and opportunities—has been a subject of human concern throughout history. However, the understanding and realization of gender equality have varied significantly across different cultures, historical periods, and societies.

This chapter provides an overview of the historical evolution of gender roles and the global landscape of gender equality. Understanding this context is essential for appreciating contemporary gender issues and formulating effective policies and interventions.

2. Gender Roles and Status Through History

Throughout history, gender roles and the status of women have been deeply influenced by cultural, religious, economic, and political contexts. In many early societies, women held significant roles in family and community life, sometimes enjoying relative autonomy and influence. However, with the rise of patriarchal systems, especially in agrarian and industrial societies, women's roles became more restricted, often confined to domestic spheres and caregiving.

Ancient civilizations such as Egypt and Mesopotamia offer examples of women's legal rights and participation in public life, while Greek and Roman societies largely limited women's status. The Middle Ages saw a complex interplay of religious doctrine and social norms that both constrained and empowered women in different contexts.

The modern era brought gradual shifts with the emergence of feminist movements advocating for women's suffrage, education, and labor rights. Industrialization and globalization further transformed women's roles, as economic participation became a critical site of gender negotiations. Despite progress, women have continued to face systemic barriers rooted in historical inequalities, which continue to influence contemporary gender relations.

Notable Milestones in Gender Equality

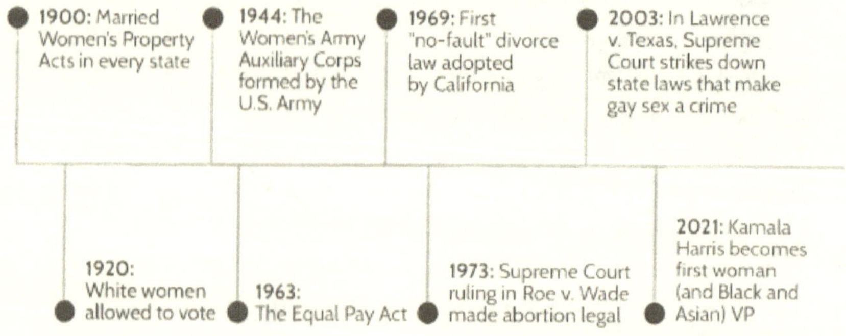

Notable Milestones in Gender Equality

2.1 Prehistoric and Ancient Societies

In early hunter-gatherer societies, anthropological evidence suggests a relatively egalitarian division of labor between genders, with women playing vital roles in gathering and social organization. However, as societies shifted towards agriculture and settled communities, patriarchal structures increasingly emerged.

In ancient civilizations such as Mesopotamia, Egypt, Greece, and Rome, women's roles were often confined to domestic spheres, though notable exceptions existed—such as women rulers and priestesses. Laws and social norms typically reinforced male dominance, limiting women's property rights and political participation.

2.2 Medieval and Early Modern Periods

During the medieval period, religious and feudal systems profoundly influenced gender relations. Women's rights were closely tied to their roles as wives, mothers, and caretakers. The rise of organized religion often codified patriarchal norms, restricting women's autonomy.

The early modern period saw gradual shifts, including the emergence of women writers, education for girls in some regions, and the beginnings of organized movements for women's rights in Europe. Nevertheless, legal and social restrictions remained widespread.

3. Women's Movements and the Quest for Equality

Women's movements have been central to advancing gender equality worldwide, shaping social, political, and legal reforms. Beginning with early suffrage campaigns in the 19th and early 20th centuries, these movements fought for women's right to vote, access to education, and property rights. The mid-20th century saw the rise of second-wave feminism, which broadened the agenda to include workplace equality, reproductive rights, and combating gender-based violence.

Globally, women's movements have adapted to local contexts, addressing issues such as economic justice, indigenous rights, and intersectional discrimination. International conferences, such as the 1995 Beijing Conference, galvanized global commitment to women's empowerment. Despite significant achievements, ongoing challenges remain, including resistance to gender reforms and the need to address the diverse experiences of marginalized women.

These movements continue to evolve, harnessing digital tools and transnational networks to advocate for equality and social justice in the 21st century.

The 19th and 20th centuries marked transformative eras for gender equality, propelled by social, political, and economic upheavals:

- Suffrage movements worldwide fought for women's right to vote, resulting in milestones such as New Zealand granting women the vote in 1893 and many countries following throughout the 20th century.
- Labor movements highlighted women's participation in the workforce, advocating for equal pay and workplace rights.
- The rise of feminist theories challenged traditional gender roles and called for systemic social change.
- Post-World War II international institutions embedded gender equality in development agendas.

4. Global Milestones in Gender Equality

Several landmark events and agreements have shaped the global agenda for gender equality. The adoption of the Universal Declaration of Human Rights (1948) recognized women's equal rights as fundamental human rights. The Convention on the Elimination of All Forms of Discrimination Against Women (CEDAW) in 1979 established a comprehensive international legal framework obligating states to combat gender discrimination.

The Beijing Platform for Action (1995) marked a pivotal moment, setting strategic priorities across twelve critical areas of concern, including education, health, and political participation. The establishment of UN Women (2010) strengthened global institutional support for women's empowerment and gender equality.

More recently, the Sustainable Development Goals (2015), particularly Goal 5, reaffirmed a global commitment to achieving gender equality and empowering all women and girls by 2030. These milestones reflect growing recognition of gender equality as essential to sustainable development and human rights.

Several global frameworks and events have institutionalized the pursuit of gender equality:

- **The Universal Declaration of Human Rights (1948)** explicitly recognized equal rights for women.
- **The Convention on the Elimination of All Forms of Discrimination Against Women (CEDAW, 1979)** established a legally binding international framework to combat gender discrimination.
- **The Beijing Declaration and Platform for Action (1995)** set a comprehensive agenda for advancing women's rights.

- **The Sustainable Development Goals (SDGs)**, adopted in 2015, include Goal 5 specifically dedicated to achieving gender equality and empowering all women and girls.

These milestones reflect a global consensus on the importance of gender equality, though implementation remains uneven.

5. Regional Variations and Contemporary Challenges

Gender equality progress varies widely across regions due to differing cultural, economic, political, and legal contexts. In some regions, such as Northern Europe, gender parity in education, workforce participation, and political representation has made significant strides. Conversely, many parts of South Asia, Sub-Saharan Africa, and the Middle East continue to face entrenched gender inequalities, shaped by patriarchal norms, limited access to education, and restrictive legal frameworks.

Contemporary challenges include persistent wage gaps, underrepresentation of women in leadership, gender-based violence, and barriers to reproductive health and rights. Additionally, the digital divide limits women's access to information and economic opportunities in many low-income regions. Migration, conflict, and climate change further exacerbate vulnerabilities for women in marginalized communities.

Addressing these disparities requires tailored, context-specific policies that respect cultural diversity while advancing universal human rights and gender justice.

Despite international commitments, gender equality varies widely across regions, shaped by cultural, economic, and political contexts:

- In **Nordic countries**, progressive policies have led to some of the highest gender equality indices worldwide.
- Many countries in **Sub-Saharan Africa and South Asia** face challenges such as child marriage, gender-based violence, and limited educational opportunities for girls.
- **Middle Eastern** societies exhibit significant variation, with some nations implementing reforms while others maintain restrictive gender norms.
- The **digital divide** and access to technology remain critical challenges for women globally.

These disparities highlight the need for context-specific approaches grounded in local realities and intersectional understandings.

6. Intersectionality and Inclusive Gender Equality

Intersectionality, a concept introduced by Kimberlé Crenshaw, is vital to understanding the complex and varied experiences of gender inequality. It highlights how overlapping identities—such as race, class, ethnicity, caste, disability, and sexual orientation—intersect to shape unique forms of discrimination and privilege. Recognizing these multiple layers is essential for developing inclusive gender equality strategies that address the needs of all women, particularly those from marginalized and underserved groups.

An intersectional approach challenges one-size-fits-all solutions, emphasizing the importance of tailored policies and programs that consider the diversity of women's experiences. This inclusivity ensures that gender equality efforts do not inadvertently exclude or disadvantage certain populations, promoting a more just and equitable society.

The concept of intersectionality has been instrumental in expanding the understanding of gender equality beyond a singular focus on women. It recognizes that gender intersects with other social categories such as race, class, ethnicity, disability, and sexual orientation, producing complex layers of disadvantage.

Policies that fail to consider intersectionality risk marginalizing the most vulnerable women and perpetuating inequalities.

7. The Role of Men and Boys in Gender Equality

Achieving gender equality requires the active engagement of men and boys as allies and participants in challenging discriminatory norms and behaviors. Men's involvement is crucial in reshaping societal attitudes around masculinity, sharing caregiving responsibilities, and supporting women's rights in both private and public spheres.

Programs that promote positive masculinity and encourage men to reflect on gender biases have proven effective in reducing gender-based violence and fostering respectful relationships. Inclusive gender equality efforts recognize that transforming patriarchal systems benefits everyone by creating more equitable, just, and healthy communities.

Engaging men and boys alongside women ensures a collaborative approach to dismantling gender inequalities and building sustainable, inclusive societies.

Achieving gender equality requires the engagement of men and boys as allies and change agents. Shifting harmful masculine norms, promoting positive role models, and encouraging shared responsibility in domestic and caregiving roles are essential strategies.

8. Conclusion

Gender equality is the result of long historical struggles and evolving global commitments. While significant progress has been made, the journey is far from complete. Persistent inequalities, cultural resistance, and structural barriers remain.

Understanding the historical and global contexts of gender equality helps inform effective, culturally sensitive, and intersectional approaches to empower women and create inclusive societies worldwide.

References

- *Lerner, G. (1986). The Creation of Patriarchy.*
- *CEDAW (1979). Convention on the Elimination of All Forms of Discrimination Against Women.*
- *United Nations. (1995). Beijing Declaration and Platform for Action.*
- *World Economic Forum. (2024). Global Gender Gap Report.*
- *Crenshaw, K. (1991). Mapping the Margins: Intersectionality, Identity Politics, and Violence Against Women of Color.*
- *Sen, A. (1999). Development as Freedom.*
- *Kabeer, N. (2005). Gender Equality and Women's Empowerment: A Critical Analysis of the Third Millennium Development Goal.*

CHAPTER THREE

Economic Participation and Women's Financial Independence

Author: *Anushka, Research Scholar at Sam Higginbottom University of Agriculture Technology & Sciences*
Co-Author: *Dr. Sneh P. Daniel, Associate Professor at Sam Higginbottom University of Agriculture Technology & Sciences*

Abstract

Economic participation and financial independence are key pillars of women's empowerment and essential drivers of inclusive growth. This chapter examines the multifaceted relationship between women's participation in the economy and their ability to achieve financial autonomy. It explores barriers to economic inclusion, highlights global trends, and discusses policy interventions designed to enhance women's access to labor markets, entrepreneurship, and financial services. The chapter underscores the importance of enabling environments that promote gender-equitable economic opportunities.

1. Introduction

Economic participation is a fundamental dimension of gender equality and an indispensable factor for women's empowerment. When women engage meaningfully in the economy—as workers, entrepreneurs, savers, and investors—they gain greater control over resources, decision-making, and life choices. Financial independence, in turn, enhances their ability to contribute to household welfare, participate in community life, and influence societal development.

This chapter investigates the complex dynamics surrounding women's economic participation and financial independence. It begins by defining key concepts before exploring global patterns, obstacles, and policy frameworks aimed at fostering gender-equitable economic inclusion.

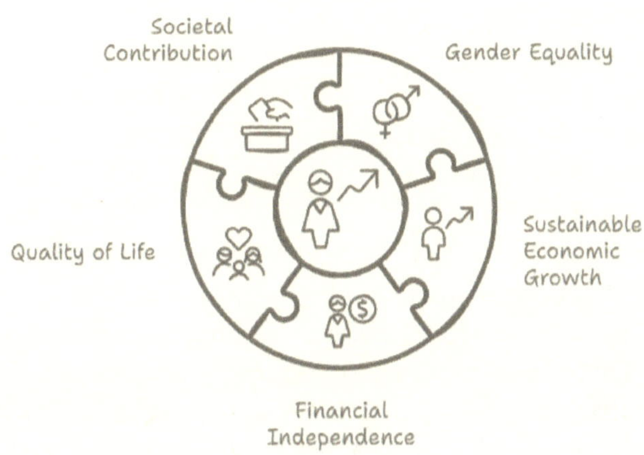

Pathways to Women's Economic Empowerment

2. Defining Economic Participation and Financial Independence

- Economic participation refers to women's active involvement in the labor market, encompassing paid employment, self-employment, and informal work. It includes not only the rate at which women engage in economic activities but also the quality of their work—such as job security, fair wages, safe working conditions, and opportunities for career advancement. Ensuring meaningful economic participation is essential for women's empowerment and broader economic growth.

- Financial independence is the ability of women to earn, control, and manage their own income and assets without excessive dependence on others. This involves having access to essential financial services like banking, credit, and property ownership, as well as financial literacy skills that enable informed decision-making. Financial independence empowers women to support themselves and their families, invest in education and health, and build resilience against economic shocks.

Together, these concepts reflect the broader goal of enabling women to exercise agency over their economic lives.

3. Global Trends in Women's Economic Participation

Despite notable advances in recent decades, women's labor force participation rates globally remain consistently lower than those of men, with considerable variation across regions.

- In regions like Sub-Saharan Africa and Southeast Asia, women's participation rates are relatively high, largely driven by informal and agricultural sectors where many women engage in subsistence farming and small-scale trade.
- Conversely, the Middle East and North Africa report some of the lowest female labor participation rates, influenced by restrictive cultural norms, legal barriers, and limited access to formal employment opportunities.
- Globally, gender wage gaps persist, with women earning approximately 20% less than men for similar roles and qualifications. Additionally, women are overrepresented in informal, part-time, and precarious employment, often lacking social protections such as health insurance, maternity leave, and retirement benefits.
- These trends underscore the ongoing challenges to achieving gender equality in economic participation and highlight the need for targeted policies to improve job quality and reduce disparities.

The COVID-19 pandemic exacerbated these disparities, causing disproportionate job losses for women, especially in service and care sectors.

4. Barriers to Economic Participation

Women's economic participation faces numerous interconnected barriers that limit their full engagement in the labor market. Cultural and social norms often assign women primary responsibility for unpaid care and household work, restricting their time and opportunities for paid employment and career growth. In many countries, legal and policy constraints, such as restrictions on women's rights to work, own property, or access credit, further hinder their economic independence. Educational disparities and limited access to vocational training reduce women's chances of obtaining skilled jobs or starting businesses. Additionally, workplace discrimination—including unequal pay, gender bias, and harassment—discourages women from entering or remaining in the workforce. The lack of essential support services such as affordable childcare, healthcare, and reliable transportation disproportionately affects women's ability to participate consistently. Finally, the digital divide means that many women have limited access to digital technologies and the internet, reducing their opportunities in growing sectors of the economy. Overcoming these barriers is essential to creating inclusive economic systems that enable women to thrive and contribute sustainably.

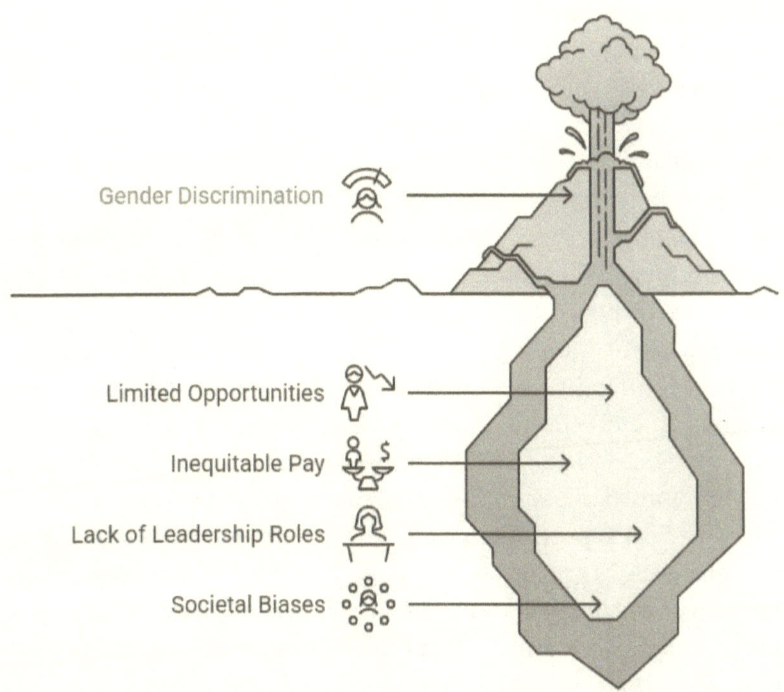

Barriers to Economic Participation

Women face multiple and intersecting barriers, including:

- **Socio-cultural norms:** Socio-cultural norms often place the primary responsibility for caregiving and household duties on women, which significantly limits their available time and physical mobility. These expectations restrict women's ability to pursue education, participate fully in the workforce, or engage in community and political life. Such norms also reinforce traditional gender roles, making it difficult for women to access economic opportunities on an equal footing with men.

- **Discrimination and bias:** Discrimination and bias in the workplace manifest through unfair hiring practices, gender-based harassment, and the segregation of women into lower-paying or less secure jobs. These factors limit women's career advancement, reduce job satisfaction, and perpetuate wage gaps. Occupational segregation often confines women to certain industries or roles, restricting their economic opportunities and reinforcing systemic inequalities.

- **Educational gaps:** Educational gaps arise from limited access to quality schooling and vocational training, which directly reduce women's employability and earning potential. Barriers such as poverty, cultural biases favoring boys' education, and inadequate infrastructure disproportionately affect girls and women, hindering their skill development and participation in skilled labor markets. Closing these gaps is critical for enabling women to compete fairly in the workforce and pursue diverse career paths.

- **Legal and institutional obstacles:** Legal and institutional obstacles such as unequal property and inheritance laws limit women's ability to accumulate and control assets, which undermines their economic security. Restrictions on business ownership and entrepreneurship further constrain women's economic participation. Additionally, inadequate labor protections—including weak enforcement of equal pay laws and lack of maternity or social benefits—expose women to job insecurity and exploitation. Reforming these legal frameworks is essential to create a fairer and more enabling environment for women's economic empowerment.

- **Lack of access to finance:** Lack of access to finance remains a major hurdle for women entrepreneurs, who often struggle to obtain credit, provide collateral, and access essential financial services. Gender biases in lending, limited financial literacy, and the absence of tailored financial products further restrict women's ability to start or expand businesses. This financial exclusion limits women's economic growth and their capacity to contribute fully to local and national economies.

These barriers reinforce economic inequalities and restrict women's ability to achieve financial autonomy.

5. Women's Entrepreneurship and Financial Independence

Entrepreneurship is a critical avenue for women's economic empowerment, enabling income generation, leadership, and innovation. Globally:

- Women entrepreneurs represent approximately 30% of business owners, though their enterprises tend to be smaller and less capitalized.
- Access to microfinance, digital platforms, and business development services has expanded opportunities.
- However, women often encounter discriminatory credit policies, limited networks, and balancing business with caregiving duties.

Supporting women entrepreneurs requires tailored interventions that address financial, regulatory, and social challenges.

6. Policy Interventions and Best Practices

Effective policies to boost women's economic participation and financial independence include:

- **Gender-responsive labor laws:** Gender-responsive labor laws play a crucial role in promoting workplace equality by enforcing measures such as equal pay for equal work, maternity and parental protections, and strong anti-discrimination policies. These laws help create safer, fairer work environments that support women's sustained participation in the labor force. Effective implementation and enforcement are essential to address systemic gender biases and ensure that women can balance work and family responsibilities without facing penalties or discrimination.
- **Skills development programs:** Skills development programs that focus on digital literacy, STEM education, and vocational training are vital for enhancing women's employability and economic empowerment. By equipping women with technical skills and knowledge relevant to the modern economy, these programs help bridge gender gaps in high-demand sectors. Targeted training also boosts women's confidence, entrepreneurship potential, and ability to adapt to rapidly changing labor markets.
- **Financial inclusion initiatives:** Financial inclusion initiatives aim to expand women's access to essential banking services, credit, savings,

and insurance products. These efforts reduce barriers caused by lack of documentation, collateral, or gender biases in financial institutions. By providing tailored financial products and improving financial literacy, such initiatives empower women to manage resources effectively, invest in businesses, and build economic resilience.

- **Social protection schemes:** Social protection schemes such as affordable childcare services, paid parental leave, and income support play a critical role in reducing women's unpaid care burdens. By easing the demands of caregiving, these measures enable women to participate more fully and consistently in the workforce. Comprehensive social protections contribute to greater economic security and help balance work-family responsibilities, promoting gender equality in both the home and workplace.

- **Promoting women's leadership:** Promoting women's leadership through measures such as gender quotas and mentorship programs in corporate and political sectors is essential to increasing women's representation in decision-making roles. Quotas help break structural barriers by ensuring minimum levels of participation, while mentorship and leadership training empower women with the skills, networks, and confidence needed to succeed. Enhanced women's leadership fosters more inclusive policies and workplace cultures, driving broader gender equality.

Countries like Rwanda, Sweden, and Canada exemplify integrated approaches fostering women's economic empowerment.

7. The Role of Technology

Digital technologies have emerged as powerful enablers for women's economic participation:

- Mobile banking and fintech increase financial inclusion in underserved areas.
- E-commerce and remote work create flexible employment opportunities.
- Online education and networking platforms support skill development and business growth.

However, closing the digital gender gap is essential to ensure equitable benefits from technological advancements.

8. Conclusion

Economic participation and financial independence are critical to women's empowerment and broader social progress. While challenges remain significant, concerted policy efforts, technological innovation, and cultural change offer pathways to greater inclusion.

Empowering women economically leads to improved household welfare, enhanced economic resilience, and more equitable societies. This chapter underscores the urgent need for multidimensional strategies that address structural barriers and create enabling environments where women can thrive financially.

References

- *World Bank. (2023). Women, Business and the Law.*
- *ILO. (2024). Global Employment Trends for Women.*
- *UN Women. (2022). Progress on the Sustainable Development Goals: The Gender Snapshot.*
- *Kabeer, N. (2012). Women's Economic Empowerment and Inclusive Growth.*
- *IFC. (2021). Women Entrepreneurs Finance Initiative.*
- *OECD. (2023). Closing the Gender Gap: Policies to Support Women's Economic Participation.*

CHAPTER FOUR

Education, Skills, and Human Capital Development

Author: *Anushka, Research Scholar at Sam Higginbottom University of Agriculture Technology & Sciences*

Abstract

Education and skills development are critical drivers of human capital formation and essential for women's empowerment and inclusive growth. This chapter examines the role of education in shaping individual capabilities, economic participation, and social mobility. It explores gender disparities in access to education and vocational training, analyzes policy interventions to bridge skill gaps, and highlights the importance of lifelong learning in an evolving labor market. The chapter underscores education as a transformative tool for achieving gender equality and sustainable development.

1. Introduction

Human capital—comprising knowledge, skills, health, and abilities—is a fundamental resource for economic growth and societal progress. Education and skills development form the foundation of human capital, enabling individuals to participate effectively in the labor market and society.

For women, education is a powerful lever for empowerment, influencing economic opportunities, health outcomes, and political participation. Despite advances, gender gaps persist in educational access and quality, especially in low-income and marginalized communities.

This chapter explores the intersection of education, skills, and human capital development, emphasizing their critical role in fostering gender equality and inclusive growth.

2. Education and Women's Empowerment

Education is a foundational pillar for women's empowerment, providing the knowledge, skills, and confidence necessary for personal and economic development. Access to quality education enhances women's opportunities in the labor market, enabling greater economic participation and financial independence. Beyond employment, education fosters critical thinking and awareness of rights, empowering women to challenge discriminatory norms and participate actively in social and political life.

Moreover, educating girls has far-reaching intergenerational benefits, including improved health outcomes and educational attainment for future generations. However, barriers such as poverty, gender biases, early marriage, and inadequate infrastructure continue to limit girls' access to education in many regions. Addressing these challenges through targeted policies and inclusive learning environments is essential to realizing the full potential of education as a tool for women's empowerment.

Education is widely recognized as a key determinant of women's empowerment. It enhances women's:

- **Economic opportunities:** Educated women are more likely to access diverse economic opportunities, including formal employment, higher wages, and entrepreneurship. Education equips women with the skills and qualifications needed to compete in the labor market, improving their job prospects and earning potential. Moreover, education fosters critical thinking and confidence, enabling women to innovate and take entrepreneurial risks, which contributes to economic growth and community development.
- **Health and wellbeing:** Education significantly contributes to improved health and wellbeing for women and their families. Educated women tend to have lower fertility rates and make informed decisions about family planning. They are also more likely to access healthcare services, leading to better maternal and child health outcomes. Additionally, education raises awareness about nutrition, hygiene, and disease prevention, which enhances overall community health and contributes to breaking cycles of poverty.
- **Political participation:** Education empowers women by increasing their awareness of their rights and enhancing their ability to engage in civic and political processes. Educated women are more likely to participate in voting, advocacy, and community organizing, and they have higher representation in leadership positions at local, national, and

international levels. This increased political participation helps ensure that women's perspectives shape policies and governance, advancing gender equality and social justice.

- **Social status:** Education plays a transformative role in challenging traditional gender norms that limit women's roles in society. By gaining knowledge and skills, women can assert greater autonomy and challenge discriminatory practices. Education also broadens women's social networks, connecting them to supportive communities and opportunities that enhance their social capital. This shift contributes to improved social status, empowering women to participate more fully in economic, political, and cultural life.

Universal primary education has significantly increased girls' enrollment worldwide, yet barriers remain at secondary and tertiary levels.

3. Gender Disparities in Education

Despite progress in expanding educational access, significant gender disparities persist globally, particularly in low-income and rural areas. Girls often face barriers such as poverty, early marriage, cultural biases favoring boys' education, and inadequate school facilities that limit their enrollment, retention, and completion rates. These disparities are further exacerbated by conflicts, displacement, and crises that disproportionately impact girls' education.

In addition to access, disparities exist in the quality of education, with girls often having fewer opportunities to pursue STEM fields and vocational training. Addressing these gaps requires targeted policies that remove financial, social, and infrastructural barriers while promoting gender-sensitive curricula and safe learning environments. Reducing educational disparities is critical for advancing gender equality and empowering future generations of women.

Despite progress, several disparities hinder equal educational attainment for girls and women:

- **Access and retention:** In many regions, girls experience higher dropout rates than boys, often due to early marriage, increased household responsibilities, and concerns about safety traveling to and from school. These factors create significant obstacles that interrupt girls' education, limiting their long-term opportunities and perpetuating cycles of gender inequality. Addressing these challenges requires community awareness, supportive policies, and safe, accessible schooling environments to keep girls enrolled and engaged.

- **Quality of education:** Gender biases embedded in curricula, teaching methods, and school environments often discourage girls' engagement and limit their learning potential. Textbooks may reinforce stereotypical gender roles, while teachers—sometimes unconsciously—may give more attention to boys or hold lower expectations for girls. Additionally, schools that lack safe and inclusive environments can further marginalize girls, affecting their confidence and motivation. Addressing these biases is essential to create equitable educational experiences that empower all students.

- **STEM education gaps:** Women continue to be underrepresented in science, technology, engineering, and mathematics (STEM) fields due to persistent gender stereotypes, lack of role models, and limited encouragement from early education onward. This underrepresentation restricts women's access to high-growth, well-paying sectors and technological innovation opportunities. Closing the STEM gender gap requires targeted initiatives such as scholarships, mentorship programs, and inclusive curricula to inspire and support girls and women in pursuing these fields.

- **Adult literacy and lifelong learning:** Many women, especially in marginalized communities, lack basic literacy skills, which limits their ability to participate fully in economic and social life. Additionally, opportunities for lifelong learning and skill upgrading are often inaccessible due to time constraints, financial barriers, or social norms. Promoting adult literacy programs and flexible learning options is essential to empower women to improve their capabilities, adapt to changing job markets, and enhance their personal and professional growth throughout life.

Addressing these disparities is vital for closing economic and social gender gaps.

4. Skills Development and Workforce Readiness

Skills development is critical to preparing women for meaningful participation in today's dynamic labor markets. Workforce readiness programs focus on equipping women with both technical skills—such as digital literacy, vocational training, and STEM competencies—and soft skills including communication, leadership, and problem-solving. These initiatives help bridge the gap between education and employment, enhancing women's employability and capacity to adapt to evolving economic demands.

Targeted training and mentorship programs also support women entrepreneurs and workers in overcoming barriers related to discrimination and limited access to networks. Moreover, lifelong learning opportunities enable women to continuously upgrade their skills, promoting resilience in the face of technological change and economic shifts.

Effective skills development requires collaboration among governments, educational institutions, and the private sector to create inclusive, gender-sensitive training environments that respond to women's diverse needs.

Skills development encompasses technical, vocational, and soft skills required for employability and career progression:

- **Technical and vocational education and training (TVET)** programs equip women with practical, job-ready skills that align closely with current labor market demands. By providing hands-on experience and industry-relevant training, TVET enhances women's employability, particularly in sectors like manufacturing, healthcare, and technology. These programs also offer flexible learning pathways that accommodate women's varied life circumstances, helping to reduce skills gaps and support economic empowerment.
- **Digital skills** have become indispensable in the knowledge economy, yet women continue to face a significant digital skills gap. Limited access to technology, gender stereotypes, and lower participation in STEM education contribute to this disparity. Closing the digital divide through targeted training and access programs is essential for enabling women to participate fully in digital economies, access better job opportunities, and engage in innovation-driven sectors.
- **Soft skills** such as communication, leadership, teamwork, and problem-solving are increasingly recognized as vital for workplace success. These skills are nurtured through both formal education and informal training programs, enabling women to navigate professional environments effectively, lead teams, and adapt to complex challenges. Enhancing soft skills complements technical expertise and strengthens women's overall workforce readiness and career advancement.

Governments and private sectors play critical roles in designing inclusive skills development programs that address women's unique constraints.

5. Lifelong Learning and Adaptability

In today's rapidly evolving economic landscape, lifelong learning is essential for women to maintain relevance and competitiveness in the workforce. Continuous skill development enables women to adapt to technological advancements, shifting labor market demands, and new career opportunities. Lifelong learning encompasses formal education, on-the-job training, online courses, and informal learning experiences.

Promoting adaptable learning pathways, flexible schedules, and accessible platforms is critical to overcoming barriers such as caregiving responsibilities and limited resources. Supporting women's lifelong learning not only enhances individual empowerment but also drives broader economic resilience and inclusive growth.

The rapid pace of technological change and evolving labor markets necessitate lifelong learning:

- **Continuous upskilling and reskilling** are vital for empowering women to keep pace with evolving job requirements and navigate career transitions effectively. As industries transform due to technological innovation and economic shifts, ongoing learning helps women acquire new competencies, remain employable, and seize emerging opportunities. These efforts foster resilience, reduce vulnerability to job displacement, and support sustained economic empowerment.
- **Flexible learning pathways,** such as online education, evening classes, and community-based programs, play a crucial role in increasing educational access for women managing multiple responsibilities, including caregiving and work. These adaptable formats allow women to pursue skill development and lifelong learning at their own pace and convenience, overcoming time, geographic, and financial barriers. By accommodating diverse needs, flexible learning supports greater inclusion and sustained empowerment.
- **Policies** that encourage lifelong learning play a crucial role in supporting women's sustained economic participation and reducing their vulnerability to unemployment. By facilitating access to continuous education, skills upgrading, and retraining opportunities, such policies help women adapt to labor market changes and technological disruptions. Effective lifelong learning policies often include funding

support, flexible learning options, and targeted programs for marginalized groups, ensuring that women can maintain their employability and contribute meaningfully to inclusive economic growth.

Lifelong learning thus represents a strategic investment in women's human capital and economic resilience.

6. Policy Initiatives and Global Efforts

Global recognition of the importance of women's economic empowerment has led to a variety of policy initiatives and international efforts aimed at promoting gender equality in education, skills development, and workforce participation. Governments, multilateral organizations, and civil society collaborate to design frameworks that address systemic barriers and create enabling environments for women.

Key policy measures include enforcing gender-responsive labor laws, expanding access to quality education and vocational training, promoting financial inclusion, and implementing social protection schemes. International agreements such as the Sustainable Development Goals (SDGs), particularly Goal 5 on Gender Equality, provide a blueprint for coordinated action.

Global efforts also emphasize the role of data collection and gender-disaggregated statistics to monitor progress and inform evidence-based policymaking. Partnerships between public and private sectors further support innovation in training and employment programs tailored for women.

Despite these advances, ongoing challenges demand sustained commitment, adaptive strategies, and inclusive dialogue to ensure that policy initiatives translate into meaningful, on-the-ground improvements in women's lives worldwide.

Several international frameworks prioritize education and skills development for gender equality:

- The UN Sustainable Development Goal 4 calls for inclusive, equitable quality education and lifelong learning opportunities.
- UNESCO's Global Education Monitoring Report tracks progress on gender parity in education.
- National policies increasingly integrate gender-sensitive curricula, safe school environments, and scholarships for girls.

- Public-private partnerships advance women's access to STEM training, apprenticeships, and entrepreneurship education.

Successful initiatives require coordination across education, labor, and social protection sectors.

7. Challenges and Future Directions

Despite significant progress in advancing women's empowerment and inclusive growth, persistent challenges continue to impede full gender equality. Structural barriers such as deeply rooted patriarchal norms, economic disparities, and unequal access to resources remain pervasive. Women still face wage gaps, underrepresentation in leadership roles, and limited access to quality education and technology.

Emerging issues like the digital divide and the impact of climate change disproportionately affect women, requiring adaptive and intersectional approaches. Furthermore, crises such as pandemics and economic recessions often exacerbate existing inequalities, threatening to reverse gains.

Future directions must focus on strengthening policy frameworks that promote intersectionality, expand access to education and skills training, and foster women's leadership in all sectors. Emphasizing data-driven decision-making, multi-stakeholder collaboration, and innovative solutions will be key to overcoming barriers. By prioritizing inclusive growth and gender-responsive strategies, societies can ensure sustainable progress toward equality and shared prosperity.

Key challenges remain:

- Resource constraints in education systems limit expansion and quality improvements.
- Cultural and social norms continue to restrict girls' educational attainment and career choices.
- Data gaps hinder the design of targeted interventions.
- Emerging technologies pose both opportunities and risks, requiring gender-responsive digital education policies.

Future strategies should emphasize intersectional approaches, ensuring marginalized women are not left behind.

8. Conclusion

Education, skills, and human capital development are cornerstones of women's empowerment and inclusive economic growth. Closing gender gaps in these areas enables women to realize their full potential and contributes to more equitable and prosperous societies.

This chapter highlights the necessity of comprehensive, gender-responsive education and training policies that address access, quality, and lifelong learning. Empowering women through education is not only a matter of equity but a strategic imperative for sustainable development.

References

- *UNESCO. (2023). Global Education Monitoring Report.*
- *World Bank. (2023). World Development Report: Education.*
- *UN Women. (2022). Gender Equality and Education.*
- *OECD. (2022). Skills for a Digital World.*
- *Kabeer, N. (2015). Gender, Labour Markets and Human Capital.*
- *McKinsey Global Institute. (2020). The Future of Work: Reskilling and Upskilling.*

CHAPTER FIVE

Women's Leadership and Political Representation

Author: Anamta Sayyada, Research scholar , SHUATS Prayagraj

Abstract

Women's leadership and political representation are critical components of gender equality and inclusive governance. This chapter explores the progress, challenges, and impacts of women's participation in political and leadership roles globally. It examines the structural and cultural barriers women face, the role of quotas and affirmative policies, and the broader benefits of women's leadership for democratic institutions and policy outcomes. The chapter underscores the importance of sustained efforts to enhance women's voice and agency in decision-making arenas.

1. Introduction

Leadership and political representation are vital arenas where gender equality can profoundly influence governance, development, and social justice. Women's participation in leadership positions—whether in politics, business, or civil society—not only reflects their empowerment but also shapes inclusive policies and equitable resource allocation.

This chapter reviews the landscape of women's leadership and political representation, analyzing historical trends, current statistics, barriers, and enabling mechanisms. It argues that increasing women's representation in decision-making roles is essential for achieving inclusive growth and social transformation.

2. Historical Context of Women's Political Participation

Women's political participation has evolved significantly over centuries, shaped by social, cultural, and legal transformations. Historically, women were largely excluded from formal political processes, denied the right to vote, hold office, or influence policy decisions. Early movements for women's suffrage in the 19th and early 20th centuries marked a critical turning point, with many countries granting voting rights and eligibility for political office.

Despite these advances, women's representation in political leadership remained limited due to persistent gender biases, discriminatory laws, and socio-cultural barriers. The late 20th and early 21st centuries witnessed growing global efforts to increase women's political participation through affirmative action policies, quotas, and international frameworks promoting gender equality.

Understanding this historical trajectory is essential for recognizing both the progress made and the challenges that remain in achieving equal political representation for women worldwide.

Women's formal political participation has evolved significantly over the past century:

- The early 20th century witnessed women gaining suffrage rights in many countries, starting with New Zealand in 1893.
- The post-World War II era saw increasing inclusion of women in parliaments and local governments.
- The late 20th and early 21st centuries have brought international commitments and legal frameworks promoting women's political rights.

Despite progress, women remain underrepresented in most political institutions worldwide.

3. Global Trends and Statistics

In recent decades, women's political participation has shown steady improvement worldwide, yet significant disparities remain. As of the latest data, women occupy approximately 26% of parliamentary seats globally, reflecting progress but still falling short of gender parity. Regional variations are notable, with Nordic countries leading in female representation, often exceeding 40%, while regions like the Middle East and North Africa have much lower rates, frequently below 20%.

Women's participation in executive roles, such as heads of state or government ministers, remains limited but gradually increasing. Efforts to implement gender quotas and affirmative action have contributed to these gains, though challenges persist, including cultural resistance and institutional barriers.

Monitoring these trends is crucial for identifying gaps and tailoring policies to promote inclusive political systems that empower women at all levels of governance.

- As of 2024, women constitute approximately 26% of national parliamentarians globally, a significant increase from just 11% in 1995.
- Women's representation is highest in Nordic countries, exceeding 40%, while many countries in the Middle East and Sub-Saharan Africa remain below 15%.
- Women's participation in local government, executive leadership, and judiciary roles remains uneven.
- Corporate leadership also shows persistent gender gaps, with women holding around 25% of senior management roles worldwide.

These figures highlight uneven progress and persistent barriers.

4. Barriers to Women's Leadership and Political Representation

Women face numerous barriers that hinder their full participation in political leadership. Socio-cultural norms and gender stereotypes often discourage women from pursuing public office or leadership roles, reinforcing perceptions of politics as a male domain. Family responsibilities and caregiving duties disproportionately fall on women, limiting the time and resources available for political engagement.

Structural obstacles such as discriminatory laws, lack of access to campaign financing, and exclusion from political networks further restrict women's political opportunities. Violence and harassment against women politicians also pose significant deterrents, undermining their safety and confidence.

Addressing these multifaceted barriers requires comprehensive strategies, including legal reforms, capacity-building programs, financial support, and societal change to create inclusive political environments where women can thrive.

Women encounter multiple obstacles, including:

- **Structural barriers:** Structural barriers significantly impede women's political leadership. Gender biases often influence party nomination processes, where women candidates may be overlooked or placed in less winnable constituencies. Electoral systems that lack mechanisms like gender quotas can perpetuate male dominance in politics. Additionally, women frequently face challenges accessing political financing, limiting their ability to mount effective campaigns and compete on equal footing with male counterparts. Overcoming these structural hurdles is crucial to enhancing women's representation and influence in political decision-making.

- **Cultural and social norms:** Cultural and social norms deeply influence women's political participation by reinforcing stereotypes about leadership and gender roles. Traditional beliefs often depict leadership as a male attribute, discouraging women from aspiring to political office or being taken seriously as candidates. These norms also shape public attitudes and voter biases, which can hinder women's electoral success. Challenging and transforming these entrenched perceptions is essential to creating an inclusive political culture that supports women's leadership.

- **Violence and harassment:** Political violence and harassment against women candidates take many forms, including threats, intimidation, character assassination, and even physical harm. This violence is often used as a tool to discourage women from participating in politics, reinforcing systemic barriers to gender equality in leadership roles.

  Women in politics frequently face online abuse, targeted misinformation campaigns, and social stigma, making it harder for them to campaign freely and safely. In many cases, gender-based violence in elections is designed to silence women's voices and prevent them from exercising their political rights.

  Efforts to combat this issue include legislative reforms, monitoring mechanisms, and capacity-building programs to support women in political spaces. Holding perpetrators accountable and ensuring safer environments for women candidates are crucial steps toward fostering inclusive and democratic political participation.

- **Work-life balance:** Balancing leadership responsibilities with caregiving can be incredibly challenging, as both roles demand time, energy, and emotional investment. Many leaders struggle to meet professional expectations while also fulfilling caregiving duties, leading to stress and burnout.

  To navigate this balance effectively, organizations can implement flexible work arrangements, such as remote work options or adjusted schedules, allowing leaders to manage their caregiving responsibilities without compromising their professional roles. Additionally, support systems—including workplace policies that acknowledge caregiving needs—can help alleviate pressure and foster a more inclusive environment.

Setting clear boundaries and practicing effective time management are also crucial. Leaders can benefit from prioritizing tasks, delegating responsibilities, and utilizing digital tools to streamline their workflow. Open communication with employers and colleagues about caregiving challenges can further create a supportive workplace culture.

- **Limited access to networks and mentorship:** Limited access to networks and mentorship is a significant barrier to women's advancement in male-dominated political and business spheres. Women often struggle to find mentors who can guide them through career challenges, provide strategic advice, and open doors to leadership opportunities. Without strong professional networks, they may face difficulties in accessing high-level opportunities, funding, or influential connections.

  To address this issue, organizations and industries can implement formal mentorship programs that pair women with experienced leaders who can offer guidance and advocacy. Additionally, women-focused networking events and leadership training initiatives can help build connections and foster professional growth.

  Encouraging mixed-gender networking and inclusive sponsorship programs can also bridge the gap, ensuring women receive the same level of support and career advancement opportunities as their male counterparts.

Overcoming these barriers requires comprehensive approaches addressing both institutional and societal dimensions.

5. Mechanisms to Promote Women's Political Representation

Promoting women's political representation requires a combination of structural reforms, policy changes, and cultural shifts to ensure equal participation in governance. One effective mechanism is the implementation of gender quotas, where countries mandate a minimum percentage of women in political offices to ensure balanced representation. Electoral reforms, such as proportional representation systems, can also enhance women's chances of winning elections by creating a more inclusive framework. Additionally, capacity-building programs, including leadership training and mentorship, equip women with the necessary skills and confidence to navigate political landscapes. Financial barriers often prevent women from running for office, so providing funding and resources can be a crucial step in leveling the playing field. Strengthening legal protections against gender-based political violence ensures safer participation, allowing women to engage in politics without fear of harassment or intimidation. Political parties also play a vital role by adopting inclusive recruitment policies that actively support and encourage women candidates. Furthermore, public awareness campaigns help challenge societal biases and foster acceptance of women in leadership, changing perceptions and promoting gender equality. Collectively, these mechanisms create a more equitable political environment, enabling more women to enter and succeed in the political sphere. Let me know if you'd like to explore how specific countries have implemented these strategies!

Several strategies have proven effective in enhancing women's political participation:

- **Gender quotas:** Gender quotas have played a crucial role in increasing women's representation in legislatures worldwide. These quotas come in different forms, including reserved seats, which guarantee a minimum number of positions for women, candidate quotas, which require political parties to nominate a certain percentage of female candidates, and voluntary party quotas, where parties independently commit to gender-balanced representation.

  Countries that have implemented these measures have seen a significant rise in the number of women holding political office. As of November 2021, gender quotas had been adopted in 132 countries, contributing to a global parliamentary average of 26.9% women representatives. While these quotas have been effective in fast-tracking gender equality in politics, their impact varies depending on enforcement mechanisms and societal acceptance.

- **Capacity-building programs:** Capacity-building programs play a crucial role in equipping women with the skills needed to excel in leadership roles. These programs typically include training workshops, mentorship initiatives, and leadership development courses designed to enhance confidence, strategic thinking, and decision-making abilities. Organizations like the Center for Creative Leadership (CCL) and UNITAR offer specialized programs that focus on overcoming workplace challenges, building strategic networks, and fostering self-clarity.

Additionally, grassroots initiatives emphasize skill development and community support, ensuring women in local governance have the tools to lead effectively. These programs not only provide theoretical knowledge but also offer practical applications, helping women navigate real-world leadership scenarios.

- **Legal reforms:** Legal reforms play a crucial role in fostering a more equitable political landscape by addressing systemic barriers to women's representation. Anti-discrimination laws help eliminate biases in candidate selection, ensuring fair opportunities for women in political participation. Electoral regulations, such as gender quotas and transparent campaign financing rules, create a level playing field by reducing structural disadvantages.

  Countries that have implemented strong legal frameworks have seen significant improvements in gender representation within legislatures. For instance, reforms that mandate equal media coverage for female candidates and protections against political harassment have empowered more women to engage in governance. Additionally, laws promoting inclusive party policies encourage political organizations to actively support women's leadership.

- **Public awareness campaigns:** Public awareness campaigns play a crucial role in challenging gender stereotypes and promoting women's leadership by shifting societal perceptions and fostering inclusivity. These campaigns use media, education, and advocacy to highlight the contributions of women in leadership roles and dismantle biases that hinder their progress.

  Initiatives like Women's March and UNiTE to End Violence Against Women have mobilized global support for gender equality, encouraging communities to recognize and uplift women leaders. Additionally, organizations such as the Human Rights Council conduct awareness programs that focus on empowering women through education, legal rights advocacy, and leadership training.

- **Support networks and alliances:** Support networks and alliances, such as women's caucuses and cross-party coalitions, play a vital role in strengthening women's collective influence in politics. Women's caucuses bring together female legislators across party lines to advocate for gender equality and push for policies that benefit women's representation. These groups provide peer support, mentorship, and strategic collaboration, helping women navigate political challenges and amplify their voices in decision-making processes.

Cross-party coalitions further enhance women's political impact by fostering bipartisan cooperation on key issues, ensuring that gender-focused policies receive broad support. These alliances have been instrumental in advancing legislative reforms, gender-sensitive policies, and protections against political violence. Countries with strong women's caucuses have seen significant progress in gender equality legislation and increased female participation in governance.

Countries such as Rwanda, Sweden, and Mexico demonstrate the impact of these measures.

6. Impact of Women's Leadership

Women's leadership has a profound impact on organizations, communities, and economies, driving innovation, inclusivity, and sustainable growth. Studies show that women leaders tend to adopt transformational leadership styles, fostering collaboration, employee engagement, and ethical decision-making. Their presence in leadership roles enhances workplace culture, promoting diversity and psychological safety, which leads to higher productivity and stronger team cohesion.

Beyond business, women's leadership plays a crucial role in policy-making and governance, ensuring that gender-sensitive policies are prioritized and implemented effectively. Women leaders also contribute to economic development, with research indicating that companies with gender-diverse leadership teams are more likely to achieve above-average profitability.

Public awareness campaigns and leadership initiatives continue to highlight the importance of women's leadership, encouraging more women to step into influential roles and reshape industries for the better. Would you like insights on specific case studies or successful women-led initiatives?

Research indicates that women's leadership contributes to:

- **More inclusive policymaking,** with greater focus on social issues like health, education, and family welfare.
- **Enhanced governance quality,** including increased transparency and reduced corruption.
- **Improved development outcomes,** as women leaders prioritize equity and community needs.

- **Cultural transformation,** challenging traditional gender norms and inspiring future generations.

These impacts underscore the broader societal benefits of gender-balanced leadership.

7. Women's Leadership Beyond Politics

Women's leadership extends far beyond politics, influencing business, education, healthcare, science, and social movements. In the corporate world, women leaders drive innovation, inclusivity, and ethical decision-making, contributing to stronger financial performance and workplace culture. Studies show that companies with gender-diverse leadership teams tend to be more profitable and resilient.

In education and healthcare, women play a crucial role in shaping policies, improving access to resources, and advocating for community well-being. Many female leaders have pioneered advancements in medical research, public health initiatives, and educational reforms that benefit marginalized communities.

Beyond formal institutions, women lead grassroots movements and social enterprises, addressing issues like climate change, human rights, and economic empowerment. Their leadership fosters collaborative problem-solving and sustainable development, ensuring long-term impact.

Women's leadership extends into business, academia, and civil society:

- Increasing female CEOs and board members contribute to corporate diversity and innovation.
- Women-led NGOs drive social change and community development.
- Educational institutions promote women's leadership through scholarships and leadership programs.

Holistic approaches recognizing leadership across sectors are crucial for comprehensive gender equality.

8. Conclusion

Women's leadership and political representation are essential for democratic legitimacy, social justice, and inclusive growth. While progress is evident, significant challenges remain in dismantling barriers and expanding women's voice in decision-making.

Sustained commitment from governments, civil society, and international actors is vital to foster environments where women can lead effectively and shape equitable futures.

References

- *Inter-Parliamentary Union (IPU). (2024). Women in National Parliaments.*
- *UN Women. (2023). Women's Political Participation and Leadership.*
- *Krook, M. L. (2010). Quotas for Women in Politics: Gender and Candidate Selection Reform Worldwide.*
- *World Economic Forum. (2024). Global Gender Gap Report.*
- *Paxton, P., & Hughes, M. M. (2017). Women, Politics, and Power: A Global Perspective.*
- *UNDP. (2022). Gender Equality in Public Administration.*

CHAPTER SIX

Gender and Health: Access, Equity, and Autonomy

Author: Ms. Anjali Wasley, Assistant Professor at Sam Higginbottom University of Agriculture Technology & Sciences, Prayagraj

Abstract

Health is a fundamental human right and a vital dimension of gender equality and women's empowerment. This chapter explores how gender shapes health outcomes through access to services, equity in care, and personal autonomy over health decisions. It highlights disparities faced by women globally, examines social determinants and structural barriers, and discusses policy frameworks aimed at achieving gender-responsive health systems. The chapter emphasizes the importance of empowering women with control over their health to foster inclusive growth and well-being.

1. Introduction

Health is central to human development and women's empowerment. Gender profoundly influences health experiences and outcomes through biological, social, and economic factors. Women often face distinct health challenges, including reproductive health needs, greater exposure to violence, and limited access to quality healthcare.

This chapter investigates gender-related health issues, focusing on three key dimensions: access to health services, equity in care, and autonomy in health decisions. It underscores the necessity of gender-sensitive health policies to promote equitable and inclusive health outcomes.

2. Gender and Health Disparities

Gender and health disparities refer to the unequal access to healthcare, differences in health outcomes, and systemic biases that affect individuals based on gender. Women, for example, often face barriers such as limited access to reproductive healthcare, underrepresentation in medical research, and gender biases in diagnosis and treatment. Studies show that women tend to live longer than men but spend more years in poor health due to delayed diagnoses and inadequate treatment for gender-specific conditions.

Additionally, societal norms and economic inequalities contribute to disparities in healthcare access, particularly in low-income communities. Women and girls in many regions struggle with restricted access to sanitation, maternal healthcare, and preventive screenings, which can lead to higher rates of illness and mortality.

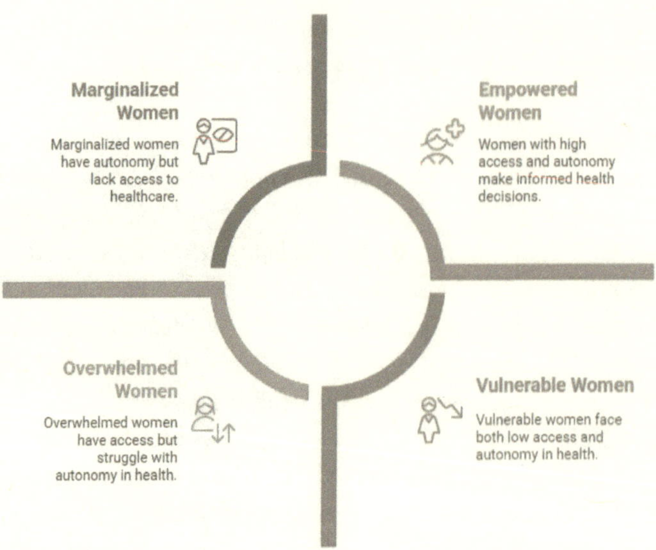

Gender Disparities in Health

Gender-based health disparities manifest in various ways:

- **Maternal health risks** remain high in many regions due to inadequate prenatal, childbirth, and postnatal care.
- **Reproductive health services,** including contraception and safe abortion, are often inaccessible or restricted.

- **Non-communicable diseases (NCDs)** and mental health conditions frequently go undiagnosed or untreated in women.
- **Gender-based violence (GBV)** severely impacts physical and psychological health.
- Women's health is further affected by intersecting factors such as poverty, ethnicity, disability, and geography.

Understanding these disparities is critical to designing targeted interventions.

3. Access to Health Services

Access to health services is a fundamental aspect of public health, ensuring that individuals receive timely and adequate medical care. However, many barriers—such as economic constraints, geographic limitations, and systemic inequalities—prevent people from accessing essential healthcare. In regions like Uttar Pradesh, initiatives such as Ayushman Bharat-Pradhan Mantri Jan Arogya Yojana (PM-JAY) aim to improve healthcare accessibility by providing financial protection and hospitalization coverage for vulnerable populations.

Globally, organizations like the World Health Organization (WHO) work to identify barriers to healthcare access and implement evidence-based solutions to expand coverage while maintaining high-quality care. Strong health systems integrate primary, secondary, and tertiary care, ensuring that preventive services, emergency response, and specialized treatments are available to all.

Local governments also play a crucial role in improving healthcare access. In Gautam Buddha Nagar, for example, the health department provides ambulance services, maternal healthcare, and vaccination programs to enhance medical support for residents.

Access to health services for women is hindered by multiple barriers:

- **Economic constraints** limit affordability of care and medicines.
- **Geographical barriers** restrict availability of facilities, especially in rural areas.
- **Cultural and social norms** can discourage or prevent women from seeking care.
- **Health system deficiencies** such as inadequate female health workers and lack of privacy reduce service quality.

- **Legal restrictions** on reproductive health services undermine women's rights.

Improving access requires multisectoral strategies addressing both supply and demand factors.

4. Equity in Health Care

Equity in health care ensures that all individuals, regardless of their gender, socioeconomic status, race, or geographic location, have access to quality medical services. It focuses on eliminating disparities in healthcare access and outcomes by addressing systemic barriers such as financial constraints, discrimination, and unequal distribution of resources.

Health equity is achieved when everyone has a fair and just opportunity to attain their highest level of health. This requires policy reforms, inclusive healthcare systems, and targeted interventions to support marginalized communities. Organizations like the World Health Organization (WHO) emphasize the importance of monitoring health inequalities and implementing strategies to close the gap.

Equity in healthcare means providing care that is fair, unbiased, and responsive to women's specific needs:

- Gender biases in diagnosis and treatment lead to mismanagement of women's health issues.
- Health data disaggregated by sex and other factors is essential for identifying inequities.
- Training healthcare providers on gender sensitivity improves quality and outcomes.
- Policies should address social determinants such as nutrition, education, and sanitation, which influence health equity.

Equitable health systems contribute to better health outcomes and reduce disparities.

5. Autonomy and Empowerment in Health Decisions

Autonomy and empowerment in health decisions are essential for ensuring individuals have control over their own well-being. When people, especially women, have the ability to make informed choices about their healthcare, they experience better health outcomes and greater personal dignity. Autonomy in health means having the right to decide on treatments, preventive care, and lifestyle choices without coercion, while empowerment involves access to education, resources, and supportive policies that enable informed decision-making.

However, many barriers—such as societal norms, financial constraints, and limited access to healthcare information—can restrict autonomy in health decisions. Studies highlight that women, in particular, face challenges in making independent healthcare choices due to cultural expectations and systemic inequalities. Efforts to improve autonomy include legal protections, health education programs, and community-based initiatives that promote informed decision-making and equitable healthcare access.

Autonomy in health refers to women's ability to make informed decisions about their bodies and healthcare:

- Informed consent and privacy are fundamental rights often violated.
- Empowerment includes education on sexual and reproductive health, enabling choice and negotiation.
- Family and community dynamics can either support or constrain autonomy.
- Legal frameworks protecting reproductive rights and freedom from coercion are vital.

Enhancing autonomy strengthens women's control over their health and life trajectories.

6. Policy Frameworks and Global Initiatives

Policy frameworks and global initiatives play a crucial role in shaping sustainable development, governance, and international cooperation. Several frameworks guide global efforts to address pressing challenges, including the 2030 Agenda for Sustainable Development, which outlines 17 Sustainable Development Goals (SDGs) aimed at promoting prosperity, equality, and environmental sustainability. The Paris Agreement focuses on climate action, setting targets to limit global temperature rise and reduce carbon emissions. Additionally, the Sendai Framework for Disaster Risk Reduction strengthens resilience against natural disasters and enhances preparedness.

Global initiatives such as UNDP's Climate Promise support countries in increasing their climate commitments, while programs like MAPS (Mainstreaming, Acceleration, and Policy Support) help nations integrate SDGs into their policies. These frameworks and initiatives collectively drive progress toward a more equitable and sustainable world.

International commitments emphasize gender-responsive health:

- The Sustainable Development Goal 3 aims to ensure healthy lives and promote well-being for all, with a focus on maternal health and universal health coverage.
- The WHO Gender Policy advocates integrating gender analysis into health programs.
- National policies increasingly prioritize reproductive health, gender-based violence prevention, and mental health services.
- Community-based interventions and women-led health organizations play key roles in expanding reach and relevance.

Effective implementation and monitoring are critical to progress.

7. Challenges and Future Directions

Women in leadership continue to face systemic challenges that hinder their advancement, but emerging trends offer promising directions for the future. Persistent gender bias, underrepresentation in executive roles, and work-life balance struggles remain significant obstacles. Many women encounter unconscious bias in hiring and promotions, limiting their access to leadership positions. Additionally, industries like STEM and finance still see lower female representation at senior levels.

However, the future of women in leadership is evolving with mentorship programs, leadership development initiatives, and inclusive workplace policies. Organizations are increasingly recognizing the value of diverse leadership, leading to more gender-inclusive hiring practices and flexible work arrangements. The rise of women-led networks and advocacy groups is also fostering stronger support systems for aspiring female leaders.

Significant challenges remain:

- Persistent funding gaps and inequitable resource allocation.
- Inadequate integration of gender perspectives in health research and programming.
- Resistance to reproductive rights in some sociopolitical contexts.
- Emerging health threats like pandemics disproportionately affect women's health and autonomy.

Future strategies must be intersectional, inclusive, and rights-based to ensure health equity for all women.

8. Conclusion

Gender shapes health outcomes through access, equity, and autonomy. Addressing these dimensions is essential for women's empowerment and inclusive development. Strengthening gender-responsive health systems not only improves individual well-being but also contributes to resilient societies and sustainable growth.

This chapter calls for renewed commitment to gender equity in health as a cornerstone of social justice and human dignity.

References

- *WHO. (2023). Gender and Health Policy.*
- *UN Women. (2022). The Gender Snapshot: Health and Wellbeing.*
- *World Bank. (2023). Women's Health and Economic Development.*
- *Sen, G., & Östlin, P. (2008). Gender Equity in Health.*
- *WHO. (2021). Addressing Gender-Based Violence and Health.*
- *UNFPA. (2022). Reproductive Health and Rights.*

CHAPTER SEVEN

Women in the Digital Economy: Technology, Innovation & Inclusion Growth

Author: Ms. Karishma, Assistant Professor at Greater Noida Institute of Technology, Greater Noida

Abstract

The digital age offers unprecedented opportunities for innovation, economic growth, and social transformation. However, women's full participation in technology remains uneven, shaped by persistent gender gaps in access, skills, and leadership. This chapter examines the multifaceted role of women in the digital economy, the barriers they face, and the initiatives promoting digital inclusion and innovation. It highlights how empowering women through technology can accelerate inclusive growth and foster equitable societies.

1. Introduction

The rapid advancement of digital technologies has transformed how we live, work, and interact. From artificial intelligence and big data to mobile connectivity and e-commerce, digital innovation is reshaping economies and societies globally.

For women, digital technology holds the promise of expanding opportunities across education, employment, entrepreneurship, and civic engagement. Yet, a significant gender digital divide persists, limiting women's ability to leverage these tools fully.

This chapter explores the intersection of gender and technology, focusing on access, skills, innovation, and inclusion in the digital age.

Enhancing Women's Role in Digital Innovation

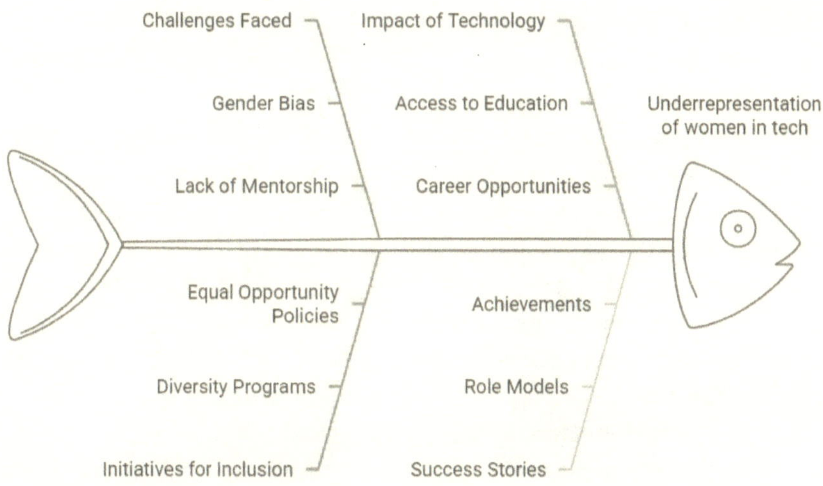

Enhancing Women's Role in Digital Innovation

2. The Gender Digital Divide

The gender digital divide refers to the gap in access to digital technologies, internet connectivity, and digital literacy between men and women. Despite advancements in global connectivity, women—especially in developing regions—face barriers to digital inclusion, including affordability issues, lack of digital skills, and societal norms that limit their participation in technology-driven spaces.

Studies show that women are less likely than men to use mobile internet, restricting their access to education, financial services, and employment opportunities. In India, initiatives like Digital India and PMGDISHA aim to bridge this gap by providing digital literacy training to rural women. However, challenges remain, as India still has one of the largest populations of unconnected women, particularly in rural areas.

Despite growing digital penetration, women lag behind men in access and use of technology:

- Globally, women are 27% less likely than men to use the internet.
- The digital divide is more pronounced in low-income countries and rural areas.
- Factors contributing to this gap include affordability, digital literacy, social norms, and safety concerns.
- Women also face barriers in accessing devices, connectivity, and digital content relevant to their needs.

Bridging the gender digital divide is critical for empowering women in the digital economy.

3. Women's Digital Skills and Education

Women's digital skills and education are essential for bridging the gender digital divide and ensuring equal participation in the digital economy. Many women, especially in rural and underserved communities, face barriers such as limited access to technology, lack of digital literacy, and societal norms that discourage their engagement in digital spaces.

Initiatives like Her Digital Skills, co-founded by EY, GSMA, ITU, and W4, aim to provide free foundational IT skills training and e-mentoring for one million women and girls by 2026. In India, programs such as Digital India and PMGDISHA focus on enhancing digital literacy among women, helping them gain essential skills for education, employment, and entrepreneurship.

Efforts to empower women digitally include community-based training, mobile technology integration, and awareness campaigns that promote digital inclusion. By equipping women with digital skills, these programs enable them to access online resources, financial services, and career opportunities, fostering greater gender equality in the digital age.

Skills are fundamental to digital inclusion:

- Women are underrepresented in STEM education and technology-related fields.
- Digital literacy programs targeting women and girls are essential to build competencies.
- Online learning platforms and community initiatives have expanded access to skills training.
- Enhancing women's skills in coding, data science, and digital entrepreneurship enables greater participation in high-growth sectors.

Investment in digital education fosters economic empowerment and innovation capacity.

4. Women as Innovators and Entrepreneurs

Women are driving innovation and entrepreneurship across industries, transforming economies and breaking barriers with their visionary leadership. In India, initiatives like Startup India have significantly boosted women-led startups, with over 73,151 startups recognized under the program as of October 2024. Government-backed schemes such as the Startup India Seed Fund Scheme and Credit Guarantee Scheme for Startups provide financial support to women entrepreneurs, ensuring they have access to funding and resources.

Globally, women innovators are pioneering advancements in agriculture, healthcare, technology, and finance, reshaping industries with fresh perspectives and disruptive ideas. Despite challenges such as gender bias, limited funding, and societal expectations, women entrepreneurs continue to thrive, leveraging mentorship programs, capacity-building initiatives, and inclusive business networks to scale their ventures.

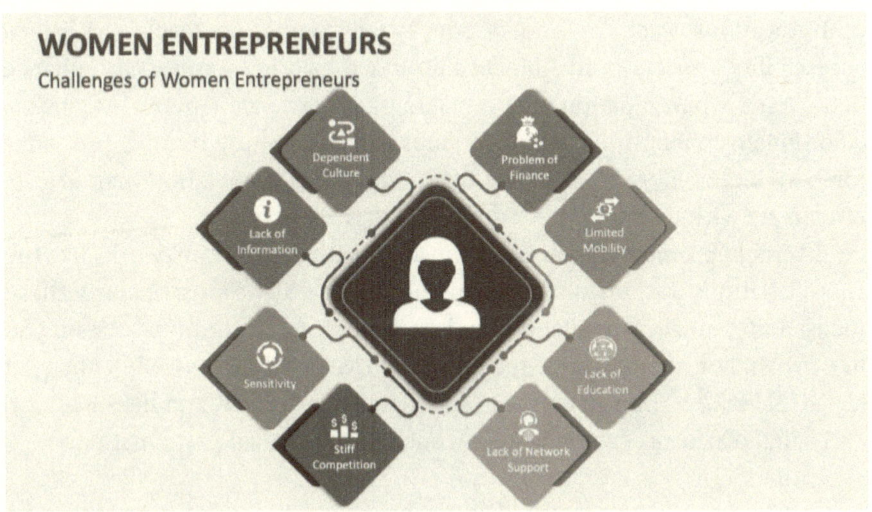

Women Entrepreneurs

Women are increasingly leading digital innovation:

- Female-led startups and tech enterprises contribute to economic diversification and job creation.
- Women innovators often address gender-specific challenges through technology, including health, education, and safety solutions.
- Access to venture capital and mentorship remains limited for women entrepreneurs.
- Inclusive innovation ecosystems require policies supporting women's entrepreneurship, networking, and market access.

Promoting women innovators strengthens inclusive technological progress.

5. Technology for Social Inclusion and Civic Engagement

Technology plays a crucial role in social inclusion and civic engagement, enabling marginalized communities to participate in governance, access essential services, and amplify their voices. Civic technology—which includes digital platforms, open data initiatives, and e-government services—helps bridge the gap between citizens and policymakers, fostering transparency and accountability.

Innovations such as mobile apps for public feedback, AI-driven accessibility tools, and blockchain-based voting systems enhance democratic participation by making governance more inclusive. Additionally, public-private partnerships and community training programs improve digital literacy, ensuring that underserved populations can engage effectively with technology-driven civic initiatives.

Efforts to promote digital inclusion align with global frameworks like the United Nations Sustainable Development Goals (SDGs), particularly those focused on reducing inequalities and strengthening institutions. Would you like insights on specific civic tech projects that have successfully enhanced social inclusion? You can explore more details here, here, and here.

Digital platforms enable women's social and political participation:

- Social media amplifies women's voices in advocacy, leadership, and activism.
- E-governance and digital services improve women's access to information, rights, and public services.
- Technology facilitates flexible work opportunities, balancing economic participation with caregiving.

- However, online harassment and digital violence disproportionately target women, undermining safe participation.

Addressing risks and enabling positive use of technology enhances inclusion.

6. Policy Initiatives and Global Efforts

Policy initiatives and global efforts play a crucial role in addressing pressing challenges such as climate change, economic inequality, and sustainable development. Organizations like the United Nations Development Programme (UNDP) implement frameworks such as the 2030 Agenda for Sustainable Development, which outlines 17 Sustainable Development Goals (SDGs) aimed at fostering global progress.

One notable initiative is the Climate Promise, which supports countries in enhancing their climate commitments through policies focused on energy, forests, water, resilience, and agriculture. Additionally, the Mainstreaming, Acceleration, and Policy Support (MAPS) program helps nations integrate SDGs into their governance structures, ensuring long-term sustainability.

Global and national policies play a vital role:

- The UN's EQUALS Global Partnership promotes gender equality in digital access and skills.
- Many countries have launched digital inclusion programs targeting women and girls.
- Public-private partnerships advance infrastructure, training, and entrepreneurship support.
- Gender-responsive digital policies integrate data collection, safety, and equity considerations.

Effective governance ensures technology benefits all genders equitably.

7. Challenges and Future Directions

Technology-driven social inclusion faces several challenges, including digital inequalities, accessibility barriers, and policy gaps that hinder equitable participation. Many marginalized communities struggle with limited internet access, lack of digital literacy, and affordability issues, preventing them from fully engaging in civic and economic opportunities. Additionally, bias in AI algorithms and data privacy concerns pose risks to fair representation and security.

Future directions focus on expanding digital infrastructure, enhancing inclusive policies, and fostering ethical AI development. Governments and organizations are working to bridge the digital divide through affordable internet programs, community-based digital literacy initiatives, and regulatory frameworks that ensure equitable access. Emerging technologies like AI-driven accessibility tools, blockchain for secure digital identities, and open-data platforms are shaping a more inclusive digital future.

Key challenges remain:

- Persistent stereotypes and biases limit women's tech participation.
- Inadequate infrastructure and affordability issues impede access.
- Gender-blind technology design may exclude women's needs.
- Emerging technologies such as AI and automation risk reinforcing inequalities without deliberate inclusion efforts.

Future strategies must prioritize intersectional, rights-based approaches to digital inclusion.

8. Conclusion

Women's empowerment in the digital age is both a challenge and an opportunity. Ensuring women's full participation in technology, innovation, and the digital economy is critical for inclusive growth and social equity.

By investing in access, skills, entrepreneurship, and safe digital environments, societies can harness the transformative potential of technology to foster gender equality and sustainable development.

References

- *ITU. (2023). Measuring Digital Development: Facts and Figures.*
- *UN Women. (2022). Gender Equality in the Digital Age.*
- *World Economic Forum. (2023). Global Gender Gap Report.*
- *EQUALS Global Partnership. (2021). Digital Inclusion Report.*
- *GSMA. (2022). The Mobile Gender Gap Report.*
- *OECD. (2023). Women in STEM and Digital Economy.*

CHAPTER EIGHT

Legal Frameworks and Policy Interventions for Gender Equality

Author: *Dr. Sunil Kadyan, Associate Professor at the School of Management & Commerce, Manav Rachna University, Faridabad*

Abstract

Achieving gender equality requires robust legal frameworks and proactive policy interventions that dismantle discrimination and promote equal rights and opportunities. This chapter examines the evolution of gender equality laws, analyzes key international and national legal instruments, and explores the role of public policies in advancing women's empowerment. It also discusses challenges in implementation and highlights best practices for creating enabling environments that foster inclusion and social justice.

1. Introduction

Gender equality is enshrined as a fundamental human right and is essential for sustainable development. Legal frameworks provide the backbone for protecting women's rights, eliminating discrimination, and ensuring equitable participation across social, economic, and political domains.

This chapter explores how laws and policies contribute to gender equality, the progress made globally, and the challenges that remain. It underscores the importance of comprehensive, enforceable legal instruments supported by effective policy measures.

2. Evolution of Legal Frameworks for Gender Equality

The evolution of legal frameworks for gender equality has been shaped by progressive policies, judicial interpretations, and international commitments. Over time, governments worldwide have enacted laws to eliminate discrimination and promote equal rights, addressing issues such as workplace equity, political representation, and protection against gender-based violence.

Internationally, frameworks like SDG 5 (Gender Equality) and conventions such as CEDAW (Convention on the Elimination of All Forms of Discrimination Against Women) have guided nations in strengthening legal protections. Countries have adopted anti-discrimination laws, gender quotas, and labor policies to ensure fair treatment and opportunities for women.

In India, constitutional provisions such as Articles 14, 15, and 16 uphold gender equality, while legislative measures like the Protection of Women from Domestic Violence Act, 2005 and Maternity Benefit Act reinforce women's rights. Studies highlight that nations with strong legal frameworks report higher female labor force participation and lower rates of gender-based violence.

- Early women's rights movements laid the foundation for gender equality legislation.
- The mid-20th century marked significant milestones with international conventions such as:

  - The **Universal Declaration of Human Rights (1948)**
  - The **Convention on the Elimination of All Forms of Discrimination Against Women (CEDAW, 1979)**

- Regional frameworks such as the **European Convention on Human Rights** and the **African Charter on Human and Peoples' Rights** have further reinforced gender rights.
- National constitutions and laws increasingly incorporate gender equality principles.

These frameworks set standards but require continuous evolution to meet emerging challenges.

3. Key International Legal Instruments

Key international legal instruments establish global standards for human rights, security, and governance, ensuring cooperation among nations. Some of the most influential legal frameworks include the Universal

Declaration of Human Rights (UDHR), which sets fundamental human rights principles, and the Convention on the Elimination of All Forms of Discrimination Against Women (CEDAW), which promotes gender equality.

Other critical instruments include the International Covenant on Civil and Political Rights (ICCPR) and the International Covenant on Economic, Social, and Cultural Rights (ICESCR), both of which outline essential freedoms and socio-economic rights. Additionally, treaties such as the Convention Against Torture (CAT) and the Convention on the Rights of the Child (CRC) provide protections against human rights violations.

In counter-terrorism efforts, the United Nations has developed 19 international legal instruments to prevent terrorist acts, covering areas such as civil aviation security and nuclear safety. These frameworks help nations collaborate on security measures while upholding human rights.

- **CEDAW** remains the cornerstone treaty obligating states to eliminate discrimination and promote equality.
- The **Beijing Declaration and Platform for Action (1995)** provides a comprehensive agenda for women's rights.
- The **Sustainable Development Goals (SDGs)**, particularly Goal 5, focus on achieving gender equality by 2030.
- Other treaties address specific issues like violence against women (e.g., **Istanbul Convention**) and trafficking.

International mechanisms provide guidance, accountability, and advocacy tools.

4. National Legal Frameworks

National legal frameworks establish the laws, regulations, and policies that govern a country's legal system, ensuring justice, equality, and governance. These frameworks vary across nations but generally include constitutional provisions, legislative acts, and judicial interpretations that shape legal protections and rights.

In India, the Constitution of India serves as the foundation of the legal system, outlining fundamental rights, directive principles, and governance structures. Key legislative frameworks include civil, criminal, and administrative laws, which regulate various aspects of governance and individual rights. Additionally, specialized laws such as the Protection of Women from Domestic Violence Act, 2005 and the Maternity Benefit Act reinforce gender equality and social justice.

Globally, national legal frameworks align with international treaties and conventions, ensuring compliance with human rights standards and global legal principles. Countries continuously evolve their legal systems through policy reforms, judicial precedents, and legislative amendments to address emerging challenges.

- Constitutions in many countries guarantee gender equality and prohibit discrimination.
- Laws addressing equal pay, maternity and paternity rights, anti-harassment, and gender-based violence are increasingly adopted.
- Family laws, inheritance rights, and land ownership regulations critically affect women's economic empowerment.
- Legal reforms must be accompanied by judicial sensitization, accessible legal aid, and enforcement mechanisms.

Country contexts vary widely, influencing the effectiveness of laws.

5. Policy Interventions for Gender Equality

Policy interventions for gender equality aim to create inclusive legal frameworks, economic opportunities, and social protections that empower women and marginalized genders. Governments worldwide implement affirmative action policies, anti-discrimination laws, and gender-responsive budgeting to address systemic inequalities.

In India, initiatives such as Beti Bachao Beti Padhao, Mahila Shakti Kendra, and Stand-Up India focus on education, financial inclusion, and leadership development for women. Globally, organizations like the United Nations advocate for gender equality through frameworks such as CEDAW (Convention on the Elimination of All Forms of Discrimination Against Women) and SDG 5 (Gender Equality).

Recent efforts include the Pacific Customs Administrations' Gender Equality and Social Inclusion Declaration, which promotes inclusive workplaces and leadership development. These interventions collectively drive progress toward a more equitable society, ensuring that gender equality remains a priority in governance and policy-making.

Policies operationalize legal mandates through programs and resource allocation:

- **Gender mainstreaming** integrates gender perspectives into all sectors and policies.
- **Social protection programs,** education initiatives, and labor market reforms target women's empowerment.
- **Affirmative actions** such as quotas promote political and workplace representation.
- **Awareness campaigns** and training strengthen societal support for equality.

Effective policies require data-driven design and inclusive stakeholder participation.

6. Challenges in Implementation

Implementing gender equality policies faces several challenges, including institutional resistance, lack of funding, and societal biases. Many organizations struggle with deep-rooted cultural norms that hinder the adoption of gender-inclusive policies. Additionally, limited financial resources often prevent the effective rollout of programs aimed at empowering women.

Another major challenge is policy enforcement—while many countries have gender equality laws, weak implementation mechanisms result in slow progress. Workplace discrimination, unequal pay, and lack of leadership opportunities continue to persist despite legal protections. Resistance to change, both at the individual and institutional levels, further complicates efforts to create equitable environments.

To overcome these challenges, governments and organizations must focus on strong enforcement mechanisms, awareness campaigns, and leadership development programs. Would you like insights on specific strategies that have successfully addressed these implementation barriers? You can explore more details here and here.

- Persistent cultural norms and social resistance limit the impact of laws and policies.
- Weak enforcement, lack of political will, and resource constraints hamper progress.
- Intersectional discrimination often goes unaddressed in legal and policy frameworks.
- Monitoring and evaluation mechanisms are frequently inadequate.

Addressing these gaps is essential for translating legal guarantees into lived realities.

7. Best Practices and Innovations

Best practices and innovations in gender equality focus on policy advancements, technological solutions, and inclusive leadership models that drive meaningful change. Organizations worldwide are leveraging digital platforms, AI-driven analytics, and grassroots movements to promote gender equity across industries.

One notable innovation is gender-responsive budgeting, which ensures that financial resources are allocated equitably to support women's empowerment initiatives. Additionally, technology-driven solutions, such as mobile banking for women entrepreneurs and e-learning platforms, have expanded access to economic and educational opportunities.

UN Women highlights the importance of disruptive innovations that challenge traditional norms, including behavioral insights, big data applications, and strategic partnerships. UNICEF has also developed a GenderTech Toolkit to support the creation of digital solutions tailored to women's needs.

- Participatory policymaking involving women's groups enhances relevance and ownership.
- Use of technology and digital platforms for legal literacy and reporting abuses.
- Multi-sectoral approaches linking health, education, and justice systems.
- International cooperation and knowledge exchange support national efforts.

Innovative models demonstrate the potential for transformative change.

8. Conclusion

Legal frameworks and policy interventions form the pillars of gender equality. While substantial progress has been achieved, ongoing efforts are needed to ensure laws translate into effective protections and opportunities for all women.

A combination of robust legislation, proactive policies, social mobilization, and institutional accountability is key to fostering inclusive and equitable societies.

References

- *UN Women. (2023). Progress of the World's Women: Legal Frameworks and Gender Equality.*
- *CEDAW Committee Reports.*
- *OHCHR. (2022). Gender Equality and Human Rights.*
- *World Bank. (2023). Gender Equality and Development.*
- *UNDP. (2022). Gender Mainstreaming in Public Policy.*
- *UNFPA. (2021). Policy Interventions for Women's Empowerment.*

CHAPTER NINE

Intersectionality and the Empowerment of Marginalized Women

Author: *Dr. Teena Hassija, Associate Professor at the School of Management & Commerce, Manav Rachna University, Faridabad*

Abstract

Empowering women is not a uniform process. Women's experiences are shaped not only by gender but also by race, class, caste, ethnicity, disability, sexual orientation, and other identities. This chapter explores the concept of intersectionality and its significance in addressing the diverse challenges faced by marginalized women. It highlights how intersecting forms of oppression reinforce exclusion and inequality, and it examines policies and strategies that can promote more inclusive and effective empowerment initiatives.

1. Introduction

Gender inequality does not exist in isolation. Many women face compounded forms of discrimination due to their intersecting identities. The term **intersectionality,** introduced by legal scholar Kimberlé Crenshaw, captures how these overlapping social categorizations produce unique experiences of disadvantage and oppression.

This chapter examines how intersectionality offers a vital framework for understanding and addressing the needs of marginalized women—such as Dalit women, Indigenous women, women with disabilities, refugees, LGBTQ+ individuals, and women from low-income or rural backgrounds.

The Power of Intersectional Empowerment

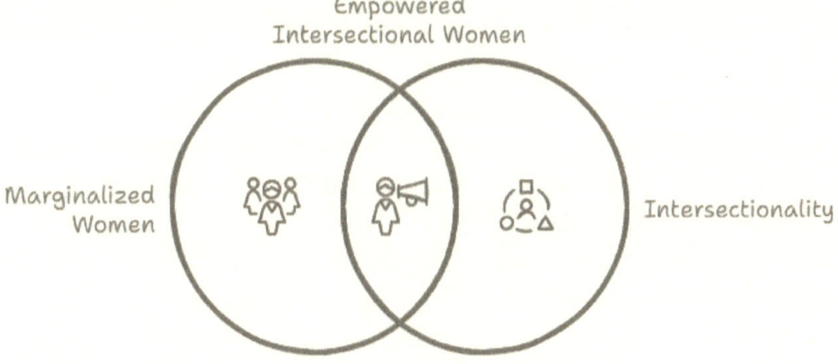

The Power of Intersectional Empowerment

2. Understanding Intersectionality

Intersectionality is a framework that examines how different aspects of identity—such as race, gender, class, and sexuality—interact to create unique experiences of privilege or oppression. The term was coined by Kimberlé Crenshaw in 1989 to highlight how traditional anti-discrimination laws failed to address the compounded effects of multiple forms of discrimination.

Rather than viewing social categories in isolation, intersectionality recognizes that individuals experience oppression differently based on their overlapping identities. For example, a Black woman may face discrimination that is distinct from both racism experienced by Black men and sexism faced by white women. This concept has been widely applied in social justice movements, policymaking, and academic research to promote more inclusive approaches to equity and representation.

Intersectionality reveals that women are not a homogenous group and that different layers of identity can intensify discrimination:

- A poor rural woman may face barriers very different from an urban middle-class woman.

- An Indigenous woman may experience both cultural erasure and gender-based violence.
- A disabled woman may struggle with both physical inaccessibility and social stigma.

Recognizing these intersections is essential to design policies and programs that are inclusive, equitable, and empowering.

3. Challenges Faced by Marginalized Women

Marginalized women face systemic barriers that limit their access to education, healthcare, employment, and political representation. These challenges are often compounded by intersectional discrimination, where factors such as race, caste, socioeconomic status, and disability intersect to create unique struggles.

Marginalized women often encounter multiple and reinforcing forms of disadvantage:

- **Social Exclusion:** Marginalized women often face social exclusion, limiting their representation in political, economic, and social spaces. This exclusion stems from deep-rooted cultural norms, systemic discrimination, and economic barriers, preventing women from fully participating in decision-making processes.

  In India, gender-based social exclusion remains a persistent issue, influenced by patriarchal traditions and limited access to education and economic opportunities. Women from marginalized communities, including tribal groups, slum dwellers, and differently-abled individuals, often struggle to gain visibility in leadership roles. Additionally, intersectional inequalities—such as caste, class, and ethnicity—compound the challenges faced by marginalized women, further restricting their access to resources and opportunities.

- **Limited Access to Services:** Limited access to essential services—such as healthcare, education, legal aid, and financial resources—is a significant challenge for marginalized communities. Barriers like discrimination, geographic isolation, and financial constraints prevent individuals from receiving the support they need, exacerbating social inequalities.

- **Violence and Harassment:** Marginalized groups, particularly women and gender minorities, face disproportionately high rates of gender-based violence and hate crimes. These crimes are often fueled by deep-rooted societal biases, discriminatory laws, and lack of legal protections, making it difficult for victims to seek justice.

Studies show that gender-based hate crimes are frequently underreported, with victims fearing retaliation or social stigma. In many cases, perpetrators target individuals based on their gender identity, sexual orientation, or perceived deviation from traditional norms. Additionally, marginalized women—especially those from racial, caste, or ethnic minorities—experience higher rates of domestic violence, workplace harassment, and public discrimination.

- **Economic Inequality:** Economic inequality disproportionately affects women in informal labor, minority communities, and those with disabilities, leading to wage gaps, job insecurity, and exploitation. Women in informal sectors often lack legal protections, social security benefits, and stable income, making them vulnerable to economic instability.

  Studies highlight that women with disabilities face triple discrimination—gender bias, economic exclusion, and accessibility challenges—limiting their opportunities for employment and financial independence. Similarly, women in minority communities encounter systemic barriers such as unequal pay, lack of career advancement, and workplace discrimination.

- **Legal Barriers:** Legal barriers often prevent marginalized groups, such as LGBTQ+ individuals and tribal women, from fully accessing their rights. In many countries, outdated laws fail to provide adequate protections or actively discriminate against minority identities.

  For the LGBTQ+ community, legal struggles include lack of marriage equality, adoption rights, and workplace protections. While India decriminalized homosexuality by striking down Section 377 of the Indian Penal Code, same-sex marriage remains unrecognized, leaving LGBTQ+ couples without legal benefits. Additionally, transgender individuals face challenges in obtaining identity documents that reflect their gender, limiting access to healthcare and employment.

  For tribal women, land inheritance laws often reinforce gender inequality. In many regions, customary laws prevent women from inheriting ancestral land, restricting their economic independence. While legal reforms have attempted to address these disparities, enforcement remains weak, and cultural norms continue to hinder progress.

These challenges require multidimensional strategies that account for more than gender alone.

4. Intersectionality in Policy and Practice

Intersectionality in policy and practice ensures that social, economic, and legal frameworks address overlapping forms of discrimination, rather than treating them as isolated issues. This approach recognizes that individuals experience oppression differently based on race, gender, class, disability, and other intersecting identities.

Governments and organizations are increasingly integrating intersectional analysis into policymaking to create inclusive policies that consider multiple dimensions of inequality. For example, gender-responsive budgeting ensures that financial resources are allocated equitably, while anti-discrimination laws incorporate protections for marginalized groups facing multiple forms of bias.

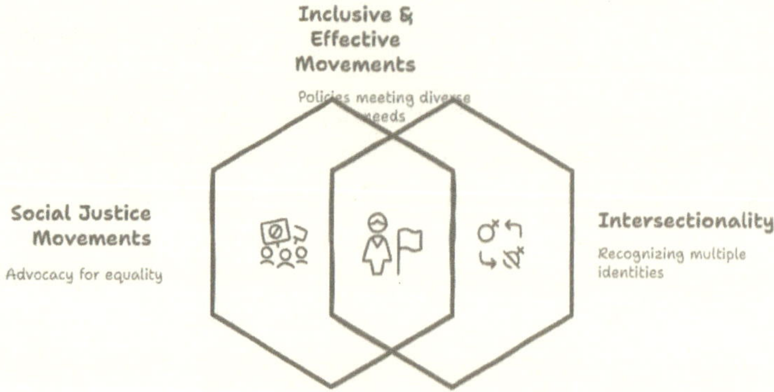

The Power of International Social Justice

International frameworks such as CEDAW (Convention on the Elimination of All Forms of Discrimination Against Women) and SDG 5 (Gender Equality) emphasize intersectionality in global policy discussions. Additionally, reports like the UNESCO Global Education Monitoring Report explore how intersectionality can improve education policies and social inclusion.

Intersectional approaches are increasingly informing policy and practice:

- **Affirmative Action:** Affirmative action policies, including quotas and reservation systems, have played a crucial role in increasing representation for women from marginalized communities in politics, education, and public service. These measures aim to correct historical inequalities by ensuring that women have access to leadership positions and opportunities that were previously inaccessible.

  In India, constitutional provisions such as Articles 15(4) and 16(4) empower the state to implement affirmative action for Scheduled Castes (SCs), Scheduled Tribes (STs), and Other Backward Classes (OBCs). The reservation system in government jobs, educational institutions, and political representation has significantly improved women's participation in governance and decision-making roles.

  Globally, gender quotas have been adopted in over 70 countries, leading to a substantial increase in female political engagement. Studies indicate that quota-mandated female representation enhances policy outcomes related to gender equality and social welfare. However, debates continue regarding the effectiveness and fairness of these policies, particularly concerning the "creamy layer" concept, which questions whether affirmative action benefits the most disadvantaged groups.

- **Community-Based Interventions:** Community-based interventions led by Indigenous, Dalit, and refugee women have proven to be highly effective due to their deep cultural relevance and contextual understanding. These programs empower women to address challenges within their own communities, ensuring solutions are tailored to local needs rather than imposed externally.

  For example, Jagrutha Mahila Sanghatane (JMS), a grassroots organization in Karnataka, India, has successfully used a human rights-based social accountability approach to improve maternal healthcare access for Dalit women. By integrating community-generated evidence into advocacy efforts, Dalit women have strengthened their negotiating power with authorities, leading to tangible improvements in healthcare services.

  Similarly, organizations like Caritas India focus on Dalit and tribal development, promoting educational empowerment, livelihood sustainability, and access to public schemes. These initiatives help marginalized women gain self-worth and confidence, enabling them to participate in governance and economic activities.

- **Inclusive Education:** Inclusive education ensures that curricula reflect diverse histories, languages, and identities, fostering a sense of belonging and empowerment among students. By integrating multicultural perspectives, intersectional narratives, and linguistic diversity, educators create learning environments that validate students' experiences and broaden their worldviews.

- **Gender-Responsive Budgeting:** Gender-responsive budgeting (GRB) is a strategy that ensures public resources are allocated equitably, addressing the specific needs of different groups of women. It integrates gender analysis into budget planning, aiming to close gaps in economic opportunities, healthcare access, and social protections.

  Governments worldwide have adopted GRB to strengthen accountability and align national budgets with gender equality goals. Over 100 countries have initiated efforts to implement gender-responsive budgeting, recognizing its role in reducing disparities and fostering inclusive development.

- **Legal Aid and Rights Awareness:** Legal aid and rights awareness are crucial for empowering marginalized women, ensuring they can navigate legal systems that have historically excluded them. Many women face barriers to justice, including financial constraints, lack of legal literacy, and systemic discrimination.

  In India, the Legal Services Authorities Act guarantees free legal aid to all women, regardless of financial status, helping them access legal support in cases of domestic violence, workplace harassment, and property disputes. The National Commission for Women (NCW) has also launched legal awareness programs to educate women about their rights and available legal remedies.

  Despite these efforts, challenges remain, such as limited outreach, bureaucratic hurdles, and social stigma that discourage women from seeking legal assistance. Strengthening community-based legal aid networks, expanding awareness campaigns, and simplifying legal procedures can enhance access to justice for marginalized women.

Intersectionality must be integrated at every stage—from planning and implementation to monitoring and evaluation.

5. Case Studies and Examples

Several case studies highlight successful women empowerment initiatives for marginalized communities. In Tarlac City, Philippines, research examined the experiences of solo parents, migrants, Indigenous women, and informal settlers, revealing challenges such as economic instability, social stigma, and limited access to education. The study emphasized the importance of government support programs and legal protections like the Violence Against Women Act to enhance empowerment. In Talluru Village, India, self-help groups (SHGs) have played a crucial role in financial inclusion and poverty alleviation. The SHG-bank linkage program has empowered women by providing microfinance opportunities, enabling them to start businesses and improve their livelihoods. The study documented both successful and struggling SHGs, analyzing factors that contributed to their outcomes. Additionally, research on tribal women in India found that education, healthcare, and livelihood programs moderately improved their conditions. However, challenges such as gender disparities, governance participation, and systemic discrimination remained, highlighting the need for better outreach and policy implementation to maximize impact.

India: Dalit and Adivasi Women

In India, Dalit and Adivasi women face discrimination based on both caste and gender. Grassroots organizations like the National Federation of Dalit Women (NFDW) advocate for their rights, combining caste and gender justice in their demands.

Dalit and Adivasi women in India have historically faced systemic discrimination, economic marginalization, and social exclusion, making their struggles distinct from broader gender inequality issues. As the lowest in the caste hierarchy, Dalit women experience intersectional oppression, where caste, gender, and economic deprivation combine to limit their access to education, healthcare, and political representation.

Despite these challenges, Dalit and Adivasi women have played pivotal roles in India's independence movement and social justice struggles. Figures like Kuyili, Jhalkari Bai, and Uday Devi led resistance efforts against colonial rule, yet their contributions remain underrepresented in mainstream historical narratives. Today, grassroots movements and organizations continue to advocate for land rights, labor protections, and political inclusion for Dalit and Adivasi women.

Indigenous Women in Latin America

Indigenous women in Bolivia and Peru have used traditional knowledge and collective organizing to fight for land rights and access to healthcare. Their struggles demonstrate the importance of cultural identity in empowerment.

Indigenous women in Latin America have played a vital role in social movements, environmental activism, and cultural preservation, despite facing systemic challenges such as land dispossession, gender-based violence, and political exclusion. Many Indigenous women have led grassroots movements advocating for land rights, environmental protection, and gender equality.

Figures like Rigoberta Menchú, a K'iche' Guatemalan activist, have been instrumental in human rights advocacy, earning global recognition for their efforts. Similarly, Berta Cáceres, a Lenca environmental activist from Honduras, fought against corporate exploitation of Indigenous lands. These women have inspired community-led resistance movements that challenge oppressive structures.

LGBTQ+ Women Worldwide

Lesbian and transgender women often face legal invisibility and violence. In some countries, community support networks and digital activism have created safe spaces and advocacy platforms.

LGBTQ+ women worldwide have played a crucial role in activism, cultural movements, and political advocacy, shaping the fight for gender and sexual equality. From historical pioneers to modern-day leaders, queer women have challenged societal norms and fought for legal protections, representation, and inclusivity.

Figures like Del Martin and Phyllis Lyon were instrumental in founding the Daughters of Bilitis, the first lesbian political and social organization in the U.S.. Barbara Gittings, a key figure in LGBTQ+ activism, worked to remove homosexuality from the American Psychiatric Association's list of mental disorders. More recently, Billie Eilish, Nava Mau, and Chappell Roan have used their platforms to advocate for LGBTQ+ rights and visibility.

Refugee Women and Migrants

Refugee women face legal limbo, exploitation, and lack of services. Intersectional approaches by NGOs provide culturally sensitive support and livelihood opportunities.

Refugee women and migrants face unique challenges related to displacement, economic instability, and gender-based violence. Women make up nearly half of the world's 244 million migrants and 50% of refugees globally. Many migrate to escape poverty, conflict, and gender discrimination, yet they often encounter legal barriers, unsafe working conditions, and limited access to healthcare in host countries.

Despite these challenges, migrant women contribute significantly to economic growth, sending remittances that improve livelihoods and strengthen economies. However, only 22 countries have ratified the ILO Convention on Domestic Workers, which protects the rights of migrant domestic workers—who are overwhelmingly women.

6. The Role of Institutions and Civil Society

Institutions and civil society play a crucial role in promoting gender equality and social inclusion. Governments, NGOs, and advocacy groups work together to implement policies, provide legal protections, and create awareness about gender-based issues. Civil society organizations (CSOs) act as intermediaries between the state and marginalized communities, ensuring that women's rights, LGBTQ+ protections, and economic opportunities are prioritized.

In India, NGOs have been instrumental in advancing gender equality, focusing on areas such as healthcare, education, and economic empowerment. Civil society movements have also influenced policy changes, advocating for stronger legal frameworks to protect women's rights. Globally, organizations like UN Women and Amnesty International push for gender-responsive policies and legal reforms to address systemic inequalities.

Empowering marginalized women requires commitment from a range of actors:

- **Governments** must ensure laws and policies reflect intersectional realities.
- **Educational institutions** should promote inclusivity in curriculum and campus life.
- **Civil society organizations** can amplify the voices of the most excluded.
- **Media** plays a critical role in representing diverse narratives and challenging stereotypes.
- **International bodies** like the UN have increasingly adopted intersectional frameworks in development programming.

Partnerships and co-design with marginalized communities are key to success.

7. Conclusion

Intersectionality is not just a theory—it is a practical lens to build more inclusive, effective, and just empowerment strategies. Recognizing the layered and interconnected nature of oppression enables us to craft responses that leave no woman behind.

To truly empower women, we must acknowledge and address the realities of those most marginalized. Intersectional feminism is thus essential to achieving comprehensive gender equality and inclusive growth.

References

- *Crenshaw, K. (1989). Demarginalizing the Intersection of Race and Sex.*
- *UN Women. (2021). Intersectionality Resource Guide and Toolkit.*
- *World Bank. (2022). Inclusion Matters: The Foundation for Shared Prosperity.*
- *Oxfam. (2023). Empowering Marginalized Women through Intersectional Programs.*
- *Amnesty International. (2022). Gender, Identity, and Rights: An Intersectional Approach.*
- *Indian Institute of Dalit Studies. (2021). Caste, Gender, and Social Exclusion.*

CHAPTER TEN

Measuring Women's Empowerment and Development Outcomes

Author: Dr. Pradeep Munda, *Assistant Professor* at Birla Institute of Technology - Mesra, Ranchi, Jharkhand

Abstract

Women's empowerment is central to achieving sustainable development, yet measuring it remains complex and multifaceted. This chapter explores the conceptual and methodological frameworks used to assess women's empowerment and its linkage with development outcomes. It reviews key global indices, national-level indicators, and qualitative tools. The chapter also discusses the challenges of data collection, cultural relevance, and intersectional sensitivity, offering recommendations for improving the measurement of gender equity and empowerment.

1. Introduction

Empowering women plays a crucial role in advancing poverty reduction, health, education, and economic growth, making it a key driver of sustainable development. However, measuring empowerment effectively requires reliable, comprehensive, and context-sensitive tools that capture its multidimensional nature.

Several frameworks have been developed to assess women's empowerment, including the Women Empowerment Index (WEI), Gender Development Index (GDI), and Gender Inequality Index (GII). These tools evaluate factors such as economic participation, political representation, access to education, and legal protections, providing insights into progress and areas needing improvement.

A conceptual framework for measuring empowerment emphasizes critical consciousness, agency, and self-determined goals, ensuring that empowerment is understood as both a process and an outcome. By integrating these measurement tools into policy development and program evaluation, governments and organizations can create targeted interventions that address systemic inequalities and promote gender equity.

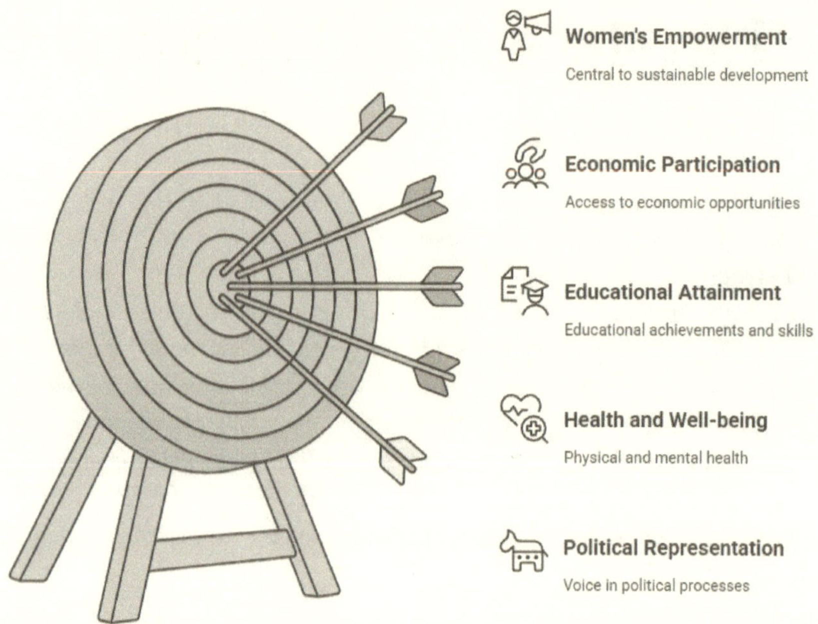

Women's Empowerment Dimensions

2. Defining Women's Empowerment

Women's empowerment is the process of enhancing women's ability to make choices and transform those choices into meaningful actions and outcomes. It involves fostering economic independence, political participation, access to education, and social inclusion, ensuring that women have equal opportunities to thrive. Empowerment is both a process and an outcome, requiring systemic changes in policies, cultural attitudes, and institutional structures. Key aspects of women's empowerment include self-worth, decision-making power, access to resources, and influencing social change. By equipping women with the necessary tools and opportunities, societies can challenge traditional gender norms and promote equality. Various frameworks, such as the Women Empowerment Index (WEI), Gender Development Index (GDI), and Gender Inequality Index (GII), help measure empowerment by evaluating factors like economic participation, political representation, and legal protections. These frameworks provide insights into progress and areas needing improvement, guiding policymakers in creating targeted interventions that address systemic inequalities.

Women's empowerment is a process through which women gain power and control over their lives and acquire the ability to make strategic life choices. Key dimensions include:

- **Economic empowerment:** Economic empowerment refers to the ability of individuals, particularly marginalized groups, to access and control financial resources and income, enabling them to make independent economic decisions. It plays a crucial role in poverty reduction, gender equality, and sustainable development, ensuring that people have the means to improve their livelihoods and contribute to economic growth.

- **Social empowerment:** Social empowerment encompasses mobility, decision-making, education, and freedom from violence, ensuring individuals, particularly marginalized groups, can fully participate in society. Mobility allows individuals, especially women, to access opportunities beyond their immediate environments, fostering independence and economic participation. Decision-making power is crucial for autonomy, enabling individuals to make informed choices about their lives, finances, and governance. Education serves as a foundation for empowerment, equipping individuals with knowledge, skills, and critical thinking abilities that enhance their social and economic prospects. Freedom from violence is essential for ensuring safety and dignity, as gender-based violence and systemic discrimination often hinder empowerment efforts. Studies indicate that restricted mobility and lack of decision-making power correlate with higher rates of gender-based violence, emphasizing the need for progressive policies and community-driven interventions to address these challenges.

- **Political empowerment:** Political empowerment ensures that individuals, particularly marginalized groups, have equitable participation in political processes and representation in decision-making. It involves legislative representation, voting rights, leadership opportunities, and policy influence, enabling diverse voices to shape governance.

  In India, women's political representation has steadily increased, with parliamentary representation rising from 4.4% in 1952 to 14.4% in 2019. However, challenges such as gender bias, societal norms, and institutional barriers continue to limit women's full participation in politics. Globally, countries like Rwanda (61.3%) and Sweden (47.3%) demonstrate significantly higher female representation in legislative bodies.

  Efforts to enhance political empowerment include affirmative action policies, gender quotas, and leadership training programs. The Convention on the Elimination of All Forms of Discrimination Against Women (CEDAW) and Sustainable Development Goal 5 (Gender Equality) emphasize the importance of women's political participation. Strengthening grassroots movements, mentorship programs, and inclusive governance structures can further advance political empowerment.

- **Psychological empowerment:** Psychological empowerment refers to the development of self-confidence, agency, and autonomy, enabling individuals to take control of their lives and make meaningful decisions. It involves fostering a growth mindset, where individuals believe in their ability to overcome challenges, set goals, and adapt to changing circumstances. Agency, as a psychological concept, encompasses forethought, implementation, self-management, and learning, allowing individuals to navigate life with competence and resilience. Self-confidence plays a crucial role in empowerment, as it reinforces decision-making abilities and encourages proactive behavior. Autonomy, on the other hand, ensures that individuals can act independently, free from external constraints, fostering a sense of personal control and fulfillment.

Empowerment is both an outcome and a process that varies across individuals and contexts.

3. Importance of Measuring Empowerment

Measuring empowerment is essential for understanding its impact on economic growth, social inclusion, and policy effectiveness. Without reliable measurement tools, it becomes difficult to assess progress and identify areas that require intervention. Various frameworks, such as the Women Empowerment Index (WEI), Gender Development Index (GDI), and Gender Inequality Index (GII), help quantify empowerment by evaluating factors like economic participation, political representation, and legal protections.

A conceptual framework for measuring empowerment emphasizes critical consciousness, agency, and self-determined goals, ensuring that empowerment is understood as both a process and an outcome. By integrating these measurement tools into policy development and program evaluation, governments and organizations can create targeted interventions that address systemic inequalities and promote gender equity. Studies indicate that empowered individuals contribute to higher productivity, innovation, and social stability, reinforcing the importance of tracking empowerment metrics.

Measurement serves several purposes:

- **Policy formulation:** Policy formulation plays a crucial role in identifying areas of inequality and designing targeted interventions to address them. Governments and organizations use data-driven analysis, stakeholder consultations, and legislative frameworks to craft policies that promote economic equity, social inclusion, and gender equality.

  For example, in India, policies such as affirmative action for marginalized communities, gender-responsive budgeting, and rural development programs have been implemented to reduce disparities. Public policy also influences redistribution mechanisms, such as progressive taxation and social welfare programs, ensuring that resources reach disadvantaged populations.

- **Monitoring and evaluation:** Monitoring and evaluation (M&E) are essential for tracking the progress and impact of gender-focused programs, ensuring that interventions effectively address inequalities. M&E frameworks help assess whether policies and initiatives are achieving their intended goals, such as reducing gender-based violence, increasing women's economic participation, and improving access to education and healthcare.

- **Accountability:** Accountability ensures that governments and institutions uphold their gender commitments, promoting transparency and equitable policy implementation. Effective accountability mechanisms include gender-responsive budgeting, legal frameworks, and monitoring systems that track progress on gender equality initiatives. Organizations like UN Women advocate for fiscal transparency and citizen engagement, ensuring that public resources are allocated fairly. Governments can also implement scorecards and social audits to assess gender-related spending and policy effectiveness. Strengthening institutional accountability requires clear mandates, enforcement mechanisms, and participatory governance, allowing marginalized groups to influence decision-making.
- **Global comparisons:** Global comparisons allow for benchmarking across countries and regions, helping policymakers, businesses, and researchers assess economic performance, social development, and governance effectiveness. By analyzing key indicators such as GDP, education levels, healthcare access, and gender equality, global benchmarking provides insights into best practices and areas for improvement.

  Organizations like the OECD, World Bank, and UNDP publish comparative reports that rank countries based on economic competitiveness, human development, and sustainability metrics. These benchmarks help governments design targeted policies, ensuring that resources are allocated efficiently to address disparities.

  For example, the Global Benchmarking Database provides internationally comparable data on economic productivity, taxation, innovation, and quality of life, enabling regions to position themselves competitively. Similarly, KPMG's country benchmarking reports analyze entrepreneurial capabilities and family business resilience across different territories.

Effective measurement informs evidence-based strategies and ensures women are not left behind in development agendas.

4. Global Indices and Frameworks

Global indices and frameworks provide standardized measures for assessing gender equality and women's empowerment across countries. These tools help policymakers, researchers, and organizations track progress, identify disparities, and design targeted interventions.

Several international tools attempt to quantify women's empowerment:

a. Gender Inequality Index (GII) – UNDP

The Gender Inequality Index (GII), developed by the United Nations Development Programme (UNDP), measures gender disparities across three key dimensions: reproductive health, empowerment, and economic status. It quantifies the loss in human development potential due to gender inequality, providing insights into how disparities affect national progress.

Key Components of GII:

- **Reproductive Health:** Assessed through maternal mortality rates and adolescent birth rates.
- **Empowerment:** Evaluated based on women's representation in national parliaments and educational attainment.
- **Economic Status:** Measured by labor force participation rates among men and women.

The index ranges from 0 (perfect gender equality) to 1 (maximum inequality), highlighting the extent to which gender disparities hinder development. Countries with higher GII values experience greater losses in human development due to gender-based disadvantages.

b. Global Gender Gap Index (GGGI) – World Economic Forum

The Global Gender Gap Index (GGGI), published annually by the World Economic Forum, benchmarks gender parity across four key dimensions: Economic Participation and Opportunity, Educational Attainment, Health and Survival, and Political Empowerment. Since its inception in 2006, the index has tracked progress in closing gender gaps across 146 economies, providing valuable insights into global trends.

Key Findings from the 2024 Report:

- The global gender gap has been closed by 68.5%, with an estimated 134 years required to achieve full parity.
- Iceland (93.5%) remains the most gender-equal country, followed by Finland, Norway, New Zealand, and Sweden.
- Political Empowerment remains the largest gap, with 77.5% still unaddressed, while Economic Participation & Opportunity has a 39.5% gap.
- Europe leads in gender parity (75%), while Southern Asia ranks 7th with a score of 63.7%.

The index provides comparative insights, helping policymakers identify effective strategies to close gender gaps.

c. Women, Business and the Law (WBL) – World Bank

The Women, Business and the Law (WBL) index, developed by the World Bank, evaluates legal frameworks affecting women's economic participation across 190 economies. It measures gender-based legal disparities in areas such as mobility, workplace rights, pay equity, marriage, parenthood, entrepreneurship, asset ownership, and pensions.

Key Features of WBL:

- **Legal Rights Assessment:** Examines laws that impact women's ability to work, own property, and access financial resources.
- **Implementation Gap Analysis:** Introduces Women, Business and the Law 2.0, which assesses not only legal provisions but also their enforcement and real-world impact.
- **New Indicators:** The latest report includes Safety and Childcare, addressing violence against women and access to affordable childcare.

The 2024 WBL report highlights that while many countries have enacted gender-equal laws, implementation remains inconsistent, affecting women's economic opportunities. Countries with stronger legal protections tend to have higher female labor force participation and economic growth.

d. Social Institutions and Gender Index (SIGI) – OECD

The Social Institutions and Gender Index (SIGI), developed by the OECD Development Centre, measures discrimination against women in social institutions across 179 countries. It evaluates formal and informal laws, social norms, and practices that limit women's rights and opportunities, providing a comprehensive assessment of gender-based inequalities.

Key Dimensions of SIGI:

- **Discrimination in the Family:** Examines inheritance rights, marriage laws, and parental authority.
- **Restricted Physical Integrity:** Assesses protection against gender-based violence, reproductive rights, and female genital mutilation.
- **Restricted Access to Productive and Financial Resources:** Evaluates women's ability to own land, access credit, and participate in the workforce.

- **Restricted Civil Liberties:** Measures women's freedom of movement, political participation, and citizenship rights.

SIGI is a multifaceted measure that helps policymakers identify structural barriers to gender equality and design targeted interventions. It is also an official data source for monitoring SDG Indicator 5.1.1, which tracks legal frameworks promoting gender equality.

5. National and Sectoral Indicators

National and sectoral indicators provide critical insights into gender equality and women's empowerment across different domains, helping policymakers track progress and design targeted interventions. These indicators cover areas such as education, health, economic participation, political representation, and social inclusion.

Key National Indicators:

- **Gender Development Index (GDI):** Measures disparities in health, education, and income between men and women.
- **Gender Inequality Index (GII):** Assesses gender gaps in reproductive health, empowerment, and labor force participation.
- **Women's Empowerment Index (WEI):** Evaluates women's decision-making power, access to resources, and legal protections.

Sectoral Indicators:

- **Education:** Literacy rates, school enrollment, and gender gaps in STEM fields.
- **Health:** Maternal mortality rates, access to reproductive healthcare, and gender-based health disparities.
- **Economic Participation:** Workforce participation, wage gaps, and entrepreneurship rates.
- **Political Representation:** Women's presence in parliament, local governance, and leadership roles.

India's Women & Men in India 2020 Report compiles gender-related indicators across sectors, offering a comprehensive analysis of gender disparities. The Ministry of Statistics and Programme Implementation also publishes gender statistics, highlighting trends in employment, education, and social development.

Governments and organizations use localized indicators tailored to their development goals:

- Labour force participation rate
- Women's access to financial services
- Educational attainment by gender
- Maternal mortality and reproductive health
- Incidence of gender-based violence
- Share of women in parliament and local governance

These indicators can be included in national statistical systems and gender audits.

6. Qualitative and Participatory Approaches

Quantitative indicators alone cannot capture the lived experiences of empowerment. Qualitative tools offer depth and contextual understanding:

- **Focus group discussions and life histories:** Explore personal and community narratives.
- **Empowerment outcome mapping:** Traces change in behavior, agency, and influence.
- **Most Significant Change (MSC) technique:** Highlights meaningful stories of transformation.
- **Participatory Rural Appraisal (PRA):** Engages communities in mapping their empowerment.

Combining qualitative insights with quantitative data enhances the richness of analysis.

7. Challenges in Measurement

Despite advances, several challenges persist:

- **Context sensitivity:** Measures may not reflect local definitions of empowerment.
- **Data gaps:** Many countries lack sex-disaggregated or time-series data.
- **Underreporting:** Issues like domestic violence and informal labor are undercaptured.
- **Intersectionality:** Measures often fail to account for diversity among women (e.g., by caste, ethnicity, disability).

- **Attribution:** Linking empowerment directly to development outcomes is methodologically difficult.

Addressing these challenges requires investment in gender statistics and inclusive methodologies.

8. Linking Empowerment to Development Outcomes

Empowered women are key to achieving development outcomes in:

- **Education:** Educated women tend to invest more in their children's education and health.
- **Health:** Empowered women are more likely to access healthcare and family planning.
- **Economic growth:** Increasing women's labor force participation boosts GDP.
- **Governance:** Higher female political representation is linked to improved governance and social spending.

Evidence from global studies confirms that empowering women leads to broader, sustainable development.

9. Recommendations

To improve the measurement of women's empowerment:

- Develop context-specific and culturally relevant indicators.
- Invest in national gender data systems and sex-disaggregated data.
- Use mixed methods—quantitative and qualitative—for a holistic view.
- Involve women, especially from marginalized groups, in designing indicators.
- Regularly review and adapt measurement frameworks to emerging gender dynamics.

10. Conclusion

Measuring women's empowerment is both an art and a science. It is essential for understanding progress toward gender equality and shaping effective policies. A multidimensional, inclusive, and evolving approach is key to ensuring that the full spectrum of women's experiences and contributions are recognized in development planning and practice.

References

- *UNDP. (2023). Human Development Report.*
- *World Economic Forum. (2023). Global Gender Gap Report.*
- *World Bank. (2023). Women, Business and the Law.*
- *OECD. (2022). Social Institutions and Gender Index (SIGI).*
- *Kabeer, N. (1999). Resources, Agency, Achievements: Reflections on the Measurement of Women's Empowerment.*
- *UN Women. (2022). Guidance on Measuring Gender Equality and Women's Empowerment.*

CHAPTER ELEVEN

Case Studies in Women Empowerment from Across the Globe

Author: Ms Renu chaudhary, Assitant professor at B.S. Anangpuria Educational Institution, Faridabad

Abstract

This chapter presents a curated selection of case studies from different regions of the world that illustrate successful models, strategies, and interventions in women's empowerment. These examples highlight the diverse pathways through which empowerment can be achieved, including grassroots organizing, policy innovation, economic inclusion, education, digital technology, and legal reform. By examining the socio-political and cultural contexts of each case, the chapter draws lessons that can inform global efforts to promote gender equality and inclusive development.

1. Introduction

Women's empowerment is a multifaceted process shaped by culture, politics, and socio-economic conditions. Around the world, diverse movements, policies, and programs have contributed to significant strides in empowering women. Studying these cases provides practical insights into what works, why it works, and how similar strategies can be adapted to different contexts.

This chapter highlights eight case studies from Africa, Asia, Latin America, Europe, and North America, demonstrating local, national, and international approaches to empowering women.

Achieving Women Empowerment

Enhanced Status

Achieving a higher social standing and recognition for women globally.

Political Participation

Encouraging women to engage in political processes and leadership roles.

Economic Independence

Enabling women to achieve financial stability and autonomy.

Education

Providing access to quality education for women.

Achieving Women Empowerment

2. India: Self-Help Groups and Economic Empowerment (SEWA)
The Self-Employed Women's Association (SEWA), founded in 1972 in Gujarat, India, has transformed the lives of thousands of informal sector women workers by organizing them into cooperatives and self-help groups

(SHGs). Through microcredit, vocational training, health services, and collective bargaining, SEWA empowers women to gain financial independence and assert their rights.

The Self-Employed Women's Association (SEWA) has been a transformative force in economic empowerment for women in India, particularly through self-help groups (SHGs). Founded in 1972 by Ela Bhatt, SEWA is the largest women's trade union, representing over 3.2 million self-employed women across 18 states. SEWA's approach to economic empowerment focuses on financial inclusion, skill development, collective bargaining, and social security. Through microfinance programs, women gain access to credit, savings, and investment opportunities, enabling them to start and sustain businesses. Training initiatives in entrepreneurship, digital literacy, and vocational skills further enhance their economic prospects. SHGs provide women with negotiating power, ensuring fair wages and better working conditions, while SEWA's advocacy efforts influence gender-responsive policies that protect informal workers. The impact of SEWA's SHGs is evident in increased income stability, community development, and policy influence, making it a model for grassroots economic empowerment.

Impact:

- Over 1.7 million members.
- Increased incomes and decision-making capacity.
- Enhanced community leadership by women.

3. Rwanda: Gender Quotas in Political Representation

Post-genocide Rwanda implemented one of the most ambitious gender quota systems in the world. As of recent years, women constitute over 60% of the Rwandan parliament—one of the highest rates globally. This political inclusion has reshaped public discourse, improved social services, and increased attention to gender-based violence and reproductive health.

The Self-Employed Women's Association (SEWA) has played a pivotal role in economic empowerment for women in India, particularly through self-help groups (SHGs). Founded in 1972 by Ela Bhatt, SEWA is the largest women's trade union, representing over 3.2 million self-employed women across 18 states. SEWA's approach focuses on financial inclusion, skill development, collective bargaining, and social security, enabling women to access microfinance, savings programs, and credit to start and sustain businesses. Training initiatives in entrepreneurship, digital literacy, and vocational skills further enhance their economic prospects, while SHGs provide negotiating power, ensuring fair wages and better working conditions. SEWA also advocates for gender-responsive policies, protecting informal workers and influencing labor rights. The impact of SEWA's SHGs is evident in increased income stability, community development, and policy influence, making it a model for grassroots economic empowerment.

Impact:

- Policy reforms on gender-based violence.
- National Gender Policy aligned with Vision 2050.
- Strengthened women's leadership in post-conflict recovery.

4. Bangladesh: Grameen Bank and Microfinance for Women

Founded by Muhammad Yunus, Grameen Bank pioneered microfinance by offering small, collateral-free loans primarily to rural women. This model helps women start small businesses, contribute to household income, and improve their social status.

The Grameen Bank, founded by Dr. Muhammad Yunus, has been a pioneering force in microfinance, particularly in empowering women in Bangladesh. Established in 1983, the bank provides small loans without collateral, enabling women to start businesses, improve their livelihoods, and achieve financial independence. Women make up 97% of Grameen Bank's borrowers, reflecting its commitment to gender-focused economic empowerment.

Grameen's model focuses on group lending, where women form small groups to support each other in loan repayment and business development. This approach fosters financial discipline, social solidarity, and entrepreneurship, helping women overcome traditional barriers to economic participation. The bank's success is evident in its high repayment rates (98%), demonstrating the effectiveness of microfinance in poverty alleviation.

Microfinance Empowers Women Entrepreneurs in Bangladesh

Microfinance Empowers Women Entrepreneurs in Bangladesh

Beyond financial services, Grameen Bank integrates education, healthcare, and digital tools into its programs, ensuring holistic empowerment. Its impact extends beyond Bangladesh, influencing global microfinance initiatives and inspiring similar models worldwide.

Impact:

- 97% of borrowers are women.
- Increased household resilience and school enrollment.
- Global replication of the microcredit model.

5. Sweden: Parental Leave and Work-Life Balance

Sweden offers one of the most progressive family leave policies globally, providing up to 480 days of paid parental leave shared between parents. This promotes gender equality in caregiving and facilitates women's labor force participation without compromising family responsibilities.

Sweden is renowned for its progressive parental leave policies and strong emphasis on work-life balance. The country offers 480 days of paid parental leave per child, with each parent entitled to 240 days, ensuring equal caregiving responsibilities. Additionally, 90 days are non-transferable, encouraging fathers to take an active role in childcare. Sweden was the first country in the world to replace maternity leave with gender-neutral parental leave in 1974, reinforcing its commitment to gender equality in the workforce. Employees in Sweden also benefit from at least 25 days of paid vacation annually, contributing to a healthier work-life balance. The country's high labor force participation rate (almost 90% among 25- to 64-year-olds) reflects the success of these policies in enabling both parents to pursue careers while raising families.

Impact:

- High female employment rate.
- Greater male participation in childcare.
- Reduction in the gender pay gap.

6. Kenya: Girls' Education and Sanitary Access (ZanaAfrica)

In Kenya, many girls miss school during menstruation due to lack of access to sanitary products. The ZanaAfrica Foundation provides sanitary pads and reproductive health education, improving school attendance and empowering girls with critical knowledge.

In Kenya, ZanaAfrica plays a crucial role in advancing girls' education and sanitary access, addressing barriers that hinder adolescent girls' development. Many girls in Kenya face challenges such as limited access to sanitary pads, reproductive health education, and gender-based violence, which negatively impact their school attendance and overall well-being.

ZanaAfrica provides rights-based reproductive health education alongside affordable sanitary pads, ensuring that girls can manage menstruation safely and confidently. Studies indicate that 2 in 3 girls in Kenya struggle to access sanitary pads due to cost and availability, leading to high absenteeism rates in schools. By pairing menstrual health management with education, ZanaAfrica empowers girls to make informed decisions about their bodies and futures.

Beyond direct interventions, ZanaAfrica advocates for policy changes to recognize menstrual health as a basic human right, fostering a more equitable society. The organization also engages boys and community members in discussions about puberty and gender equality, promoting a holistic approach to empowerment.

Impact:

- Reduced school dropout rates among adolescent girls.
- Enhanced confidence and body literacy.
- Shift in community attitudes about menstruation.

7. Bolivia: Indigenous Women's Rights and Constitutional Recognition

Bolivia's 2009 Constitution recognized the rights of Indigenous peoples and gender equality, marking a turning point for Indigenous women's empowerment. Organizations like Bartolina Sisa Confederation advocate for land rights, political participation, and cultural preservation.

Bolivia has made significant strides in recognizing and protecting Indigenous women's rights, particularly through its 2009 Constitution, which enshrines gender equality and Indigenous representation. The Constitution guarantees equal participation of men and women in political processes, ensuring that Indigenous women have a voice in governance.

One of the most influential movements advocating for Indigenous women's rights is Las Bartolinas, the National Confederation of Campesino Women of Bolivia. This organization, with over 1.5 million members, has played a crucial role in securing land rights, political inclusion, and economic opportunities for Indigenous women. Historically marginalized, Indigenous women have transitioned from being excluded from decision-making to holding leadership positions in Bolivia's government.

Despite these advancements, challenges remain, including gender-based violence, economic disparities, and political fragmentation. The ongoing political shifts within Bolivia's leadership have affected Indigenous women's organizations, highlighting the need for continued advocacy and policy reinforcement.

Impact:

- Inclusion of Indigenous women in national politics.
- Legal recognition of collective land ownership.
- Revitalization of Indigenous women's leadership.

8. United States: #MeToo Movement and Social Accountability

The #MeToo movement, initiated by activist Tarana Burke and amplified globally in 2017, brought visibility to the widespread issue of sexual harassment and assault. It catalyzed policy changes in workplaces and led to a broader conversation about consent, gender norms, and power.

The #MeToo movement emerged as a powerful force for social accountability, addressing sexual harassment and gender-based violence in the United States and beyond. Originally coined by activist Tarana Burke in 2006, the movement gained global traction in 2017 when actress Alyssa Milano encouraged survivors to share their experiences online. This led to widespread revelations about misconduct in workplaces, entertainment, and politics, holding perpetrators accountable and reshaping societal norms.

The movement has influenced policy changes, workplace reforms, and legal actions, prompting organizations to implement stricter harassment policies and reporting mechanisms. High-profile cases, such as the conviction of Harvey Weinstein, demonstrated the movement's impact on legal accountability and cultural shifts. However, challenges remain, including concerns about due process, backlash, and the sustainability of long-term reforms.

Impact:

- Legislative action on workplace harassment.
- Institutional reforms across industries.
- Increased public discourse on gender equity.

9. Comparative Analysis: Common Threads and Lessons Learned

A comparative analysis of global empowerment initiatives reveals several common threads and lessons learned that can inform future strategies. Across different regions, successful programs share key elements such as grassroots engagement, policy integration, financial inclusion, and social accountability. Community-led approaches, as seen in SEWA in India and Grameen Bank in Bangladesh, demonstrate the power of self-help groups and microfinance in fostering economic independence. Policy support plays a crucial role, as evidenced by Sweden's parental leave policies and Bolivia's constitutional recognition of Indigenous women's rights, highlighting the importance of institutional backing for gender equality. Education and awareness are central to empowerment, with initiatives like Kenya's ZanaAfrica and the #MeToo movement in the U.S. emphasizing advocacy and knowledge-sharing. Legal and financial inclusion, measured through indices like Women, Business and the Law (WBL) and the Social Institutions and Gender Index (SIGI), showcase how legal frameworks shape economic opportunities for women. Key lessons learned include the importance of intersectionality in addressing gender disparities, the need for sustainable funding and institutional support, the value of data-driven decision-making through global indices like GII and GGGI, and the impact of public engagement in driving systemic change. These insights provide a roadmap for refining empowerment strategies and ensuring long-term progress toward gender equality.

Despite varying contexts, these case studies share key elements:

- **Community Engagement:** Community engagement is a cornerstone of successful empowerment programs, ensuring that initiatives are rooted in local realities and that women are active agents of change. Programs that prioritize grassroots involvement foster ownership, sustainability, and cultural relevance, making them more effective in addressing gender disparities. Women's participation in decision-making, advocacy, and economic activities strengthens community resilience and drives long-term social transformation.

  For example, initiatives like SEWA in India and Grameen Bank in Bangladesh demonstrate how self-help groups and microfinance empower women economically, while ZanaAfrica in Kenya integrates education and menstrual health to remove barriers to girls' education. Similarly, Bolivia's Indigenous women's movements and the #MeToo movement in the U.S. highlight the power of collective action and policy advocacy in challenging systemic inequalities.

  Studies show that when women are actively engaged in community leadership, societies experience higher education rates, improved family health, and greater economic stability. Programs that embrace local knowledge, amplify women's voices, and promote inclusive governance create lasting impact.

- **Policy Support:** Legislative backing plays a crucial role in ensuring the sustainability and scalability of empowerment initiatives. Strong policy frameworks provide institutional support, legal protections, and financial resources, enabling programs to expand and maintain long-term impact. For example, gender-responsive budgeting ensures that public funds are allocated equitably, supporting initiatives that promote women's economic participation and social inclusion. Similarly, affirmative action policies create pathways for marginalized groups to access education, employment, and leadership opportunities. Countries that integrate sustainability laws and frameworks into their governance structures, such as those aligned with the United Nations Sustainable Development Goals (SDGs), demonstrate higher success rates in achieving gender equality. Legislative scrutiny also plays a vital role in monitoring policy effectiveness, ensuring that interventions remain relevant and adaptable to evolving societal needs.

- **Intersectional Approach:** An intersectional approach ensures that empowerment programs address multiple layers of inequality, such as class, race, age, gender, and disability, making them more inclusive and effective. By recognizing that individuals experience overlapping forms of discrimination, intersectionality helps policymakers and organizations design targeted interventions that cater to diverse needs.

  For example, initiatives that support women of color in entrepreneurship acknowledge both gender and racial barriers, while programs promoting elderly women's financial independence consider age-related economic challenges. Similarly, education policies that focus on low-income minority students integrate solutions for class and racial disparities, ensuring equitable access to opportunities.

  Studies show that intersectional frameworks lead to higher participation rates, better policy outcomes, and stronger community engagement, as they reflect lived experiences more accurately.

- **Partnerships:** Partnerships between governments, NGOs, and private actors play a crucial role in strengthening the impact of social and economic initiatives. Public-private partnerships (PPPs) enable governments to leverage private sector expertise, funding, and innovation, while NGOs contribute grassroots knowledge, advocacy, and community engagement. This collaboration enhances efficiency, scalability, and sustainability, ensuring that interventions address complex societal challenges effectively. For instance, PPPs have been instrumental in healthcare, education, and environmental sustainability, where joint efforts improve service delivery and policy implementation. NGOs benefit from corporate funding and technical support, while businesses gain social credibility and market expansion through responsible engagement. Successful partnerships require clear objectives, accountability mechanisms, and shared responsibilities, fostering long-term impact.

- **Monitoring and Evaluation:** Monitoring and evaluation (M&E) are essential for ensuring accountability and continuous improvement in empowerment programs. Evidence-based strategies allow policymakers and organizations to track progress, assess impact, and refine interventions based on data-driven insights. Effective M&E frameworks incorporate key performance indicators (KPIs), impact assessments, and adaptive learning mechanisms, ensuring that programs remain responsive to evolving needs. By systematically collecting and analyzing quantitative and qualitative data, organizations can identify successes, challenges, and areas for improvement, leading to more efficient resource allocation and policy adjustments. Additionally, transparent reporting and stakeholder engagement enhance credibility and foster trust, reinforcing the sustainability of initiatives.

10. Conclusion

These global case studies offer powerful examples of how women's empowerment can be realized through diverse strategies and interventions. They demonstrate that sustainable empowerment requires a combination of bottom-up participation, top-down policy reform, and intersectional sensitivity.

By learning from each other, countries and communities can adopt and adapt these approaches to their own contexts, accelerating the path toward gender equality and inclusive development.

References

- *UN Women. (2023). Global Gender Equality Trends.*
- *Grameen Bank. (2022). Annual Impact Report.*
- *Rwanda Ministry of Gender and Family Promotion. (2023). Gender Monitoring Office Reports.*
- *SEWA. (2022). Empowering Women in the Informal Economy.*
- *ZanaAfrica Foundation. (2021). Menstrual Health and Education Impact.*
- *Government of Sweden. (2023). Parental Leave and Gender Equality Policy Review.*
- *MeToo Movement. (2022). Social Justice and Legal Reform.*

CHAPTER TWELVE

Future Directions for Inclusive Growth and Gender Justice

Author: Dr. Rashi Srivastav, Assistant Professor at Greater Noida Institute of Technology, Greater Noida)
Co-Author: Mr. Brijesh Kumar, Assistant Professor at Greater Noida Institute of Technology, MBA Institute, Greater Noida

Abstract

As the global community strives for sustainable development, inclusive growth and gender justice remain central priorities. While progress has been made, persistent disparities in income, opportunity, representation, and access to resources continue to hinder women's full participation in development. This chapter outlines emerging trends, strategic policy directions, and transformative approaches needed to ensure that growth benefits all genders equitably. It emphasizes systemic change, intersectional frameworks, and the critical role of technology, education, governance, and civil society in shaping a just and inclusive future.

1. Introduction

The 21st century has seen significant advances in gender equality, yet systemic barriers and deep-rooted inequalities persist. True inclusive growth—economic expansion that creates equitable opportunities for all—must be anchored in gender justice. As societies evolve in response to globalization, technological transformation, climate change, and demographic shifts, future pathways must center on justice, inclusion, and the empowerment of all marginalized voices.

The Power of Synergy for Sustainable Development

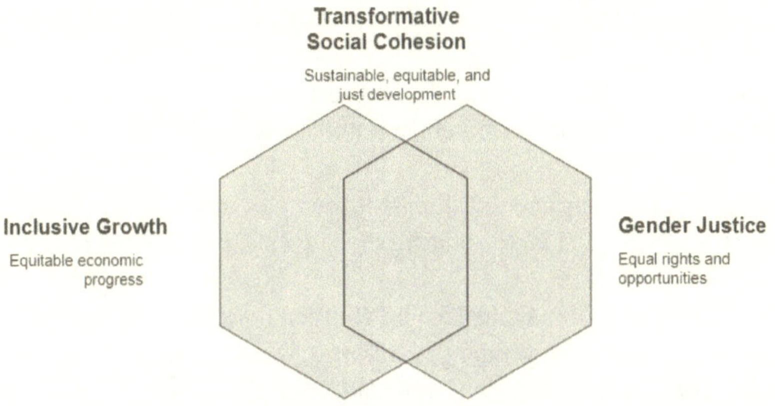

The Power of Synergy for Sustainable Development

2. Rethinking Growth Through a Gender Lens

Rethinking growth through a gender lens involves integrating gender equality into economic policies, business strategies, and development frameworks to create inclusive and sustainable growth. Traditional economic models often overlook the unpaid labor, caregiving responsibilities, and systemic barriers that disproportionately affect women. By addressing these gaps, economies can unlock higher productivity, innovation, and social stability. Increasing women's access to education, employment, and leadership roles enhances economic output, while gender lens investing supports women-led businesses, fostering innovation and financial independence. Gender-responsive policies, such as equal pay laws and parental leave, create fairer labor markets, and improving childcare, healthcare, and financial inclusion enables women to participate fully in the economy. Studies show that closing gender gaps in labor markets could add trillions to global GDP, and countries that prioritize gender equity in economic planning experience higher growth rates and improved social outcomes.

Inclusive growth requires a shift from traditional economic metrics to models that value equity, care work, social well-being, and sustainability. A gender-just approach reframes growth to:

- Recognize and redistribute unpaid and care work.
- Address structural inequalities in labor markets.
- Promote equitable access to assets and services.
- Ensure representation in economic, political, and social institutions.

Feminist economists and development theorists advocate for redefining prosperity beyond GDP, incorporating social cohesion and gender equality as essential indicators.

3. Strategic Pillars for Inclusive and Gender-Just Futures

Building inclusive and gender-just futures requires a strategic approach that integrates equity, empowerment, and systemic change. Several key pillars shape effective gender-responsive strategies, ensuring that policies and programs address structural inequalities while fostering sustainable progress. Economic empowerment plays a crucial role in expanding financial inclusion, entrepreneurship, and equitable labor policies to ensure women's full participation in the economy. Strengthening access to quality education, STEM opportunities, and vocational training helps bridge gender gaps in knowledge and employment. Legal and policy frameworks, including gender-responsive laws, affirmative action, and anti-discrimination policies, protect rights and promote equality. Health and well-being initiatives ensure reproductive rights, maternal healthcare, and mental health support, addressing gender-specific health disparities. Increasing women's participation in governance, corporate leadership, and community decision-making drives systemic change, while challenging harmful stereotypes, gender-based violence, and discriminatory practices through advocacy and awareness campaigns fosters cultural shifts. Recognizing race, class, disability, and LGBTQ+ identities in gender policies ensures truly inclusive frameworks. These pillars align with global strategies, such as the World Bank Gender Strategy 2024-2030, which emphasizes economic participation, foundational well-being, and leadership.

Strengthening Gender Equality Research

Strengthening Gender Equality Research

a. Inclusive Economic Policies

Inclusive economic policies prioritize gender equality, financial accessibility, and equitable labor opportunities, ensuring that economic growth benefits all segments of society. These policies focus on closing wage gaps, expanding access to credit for women entrepreneurs, and implementing gender-responsive budgeting to allocate resources effectively. Governments and organizations worldwide have adopted measures such as equal pay legislation, parental leave policies, and affirmative action programs to promote workplace diversity and inclusion. Additionally, microfinance initiatives and social protection schemes empower marginalized groups, fostering sustainable economic participation. Studies indicate that economies with strong gender-inclusive policies experience higher productivity, innovation, and social stability, reinforcing the importance of integrating gender perspectives into economic planning.

Policies must be designed to correct historical disadvantages and ensure women's economic inclusion. Key actions include:

- Gender-responsive budgeting and public investment.
- Support for women-owned enterprises and cooperatives.
- Equal access to credit, land, and property rights.
- Social protection programs that address women's specific needs.

b. Gender-Transformative Education and Skills Development

Gender-transformative education and skills development aim to challenge gender norms, promote equity, and empower individuals through inclusive learning environments. This approach goes beyond gender-sensitive education by actively reshaping attitudes, behaviors, and institutional structures to foster equality. It integrates feminist pedagogy, intersectional analysis, and participatory learning, ensuring that both educators and learners engage in critical discussions on gender roles and systemic inequalities.

Programs implementing gender-transformative education focus on curriculum reform, teacher training, and policy advocacy, addressing biases that limit opportunities for marginalized groups. For instance, initiatives by UNICEF and Plan International emphasize gender-responsive teaching methods, safe learning spaces, and mentorship programs to support girls and non-binary students. Additionally, vocational training and STEM education tailored for women help bridge employment gaps and economic disparities.

Studies show that gender-transformative education enhances social inclusion, economic participation, and leadership opportunities, making it a key driver of sustainable development.

Future economies will be driven by skills, innovation, and adaptability. Education must:

- Eliminate gender biases in curricula.
- Promote STEM education and digital literacy for girls.
- Equip women with leadership and entrepreneurial skills.
- Foster lifelong learning opportunities.

c. Technology and Digital Inclusion

Technology and digital inclusion play a crucial role in advancing gender equality, ensuring that women and marginalized groups have equitable access to digital tools, education, and economic opportunities. Despite progress, the digital gender divide persists, with women in low- and middle-income countries being 15% less likely than men to use mobile internet. Closing this gap is essential for inclusive development, as digital technologies facilitate education, financial inclusion, and entrepreneurship.

Global initiatives, such as the World Bank's Digital Empowerment and Equity Program (DEEP), aim to enable 300 million more women to use broadband internet by 2030. Strategies include investments in digital infrastructure, consumer financing for smartphones, and digital literacy programs tailored for underserved women and girls. Additionally, organizations like UN Women advocate for gender-responsive digital policies, ensuring that women can fully participate in the digital economy.

Countries like Pakistan and India have launched national digital inclusion programs, expanding rural broadband access, digital literacy training, and financial platforms to empower women. However, challenges such as affordability, lack of skills, and unsafe digital environments must be addressed collaboratively to achieve equitable digital transformation.

As digitalization reshapes economies and societies, ensuring women's equal access to technology is crucial.

- Bridge the digital gender divide through affordable connectivity and training.
- Foster women's participation in tech design, innovation, and policy.
- Address online safety, harassment, and data privacy for women.

d. Climate Justice and Sustainability

Climate justice and sustainability are deeply interconnected with gender equality, as women and marginalized communities often bear the brunt of climate change impacts. The climate crisis is not gender-neutral, with women facing greater health, economic, and social risks due to environmental degradation and resource scarcity. Studies indicate that by 2050, climate change may push up to 158 million more women and girls into poverty, exacerbating existing inequalities.

Women play a crucial role in environmental conservation, sustainable agriculture, and climate adaptation, yet they often have limited access to land, financial resources, and decision-making platforms. Gender-responsive climate policies, such as inclusive land rights, green job initiatives, and climate finance for women-led enterprises, are essential for fostering resilience and equitable development.

Additionally, integrating women's leadership in climate governance strengthens policy effectiveness and community-driven solutions, ensuring that sustainability efforts address diverse needs.

Women are disproportionately affected by climate change yet underrepresented in environmental leadership. Gender-responsive climate action must:

- Involve women in climate governance.
- Promote green jobs and sustainable livelihoods for women.
- Ensure access to climate-resilient infrastructure and resources.

e. Political Participation and Leadership

Political participation and leadership are essential for achieving gender equality, yet women remain underrepresented in decision-making roles worldwide. Despite progress, only 27.2% of parliamentarians globally are women, and gender parity in national legislative bodies is not expected before 2063. Women's leadership enhances policy diversity, social inclusion, and governance effectiveness, as studies show that female leaders prioritize education, healthcare, and social welfare. However, barriers such as socio-economic disparities, cultural norms, and institutional biases continue to limit women's political engagement. Strategies to increase representation include gender quotas, leadership training, and financial support for female candidates, ensuring equitable access to political opportunities.

Gender-just growth depends on women's voice in decision-making.

- Enforce quotas and parity laws in political representation.
- Build women's leadership at local and national levels.
- Promote gender-sensitive governance and accountability mechanisms.

4. Intersectionality as a Core Principle

A future-focused approach must recognize that gender does not exist in isolation. Intersectionality addresses how gender intersects with race, class, disability, age, sexuality, and geography, influencing access to rights and resources.

Policy frameworks should disaggregate data, consult marginalized groups, and design inclusive interventions that reach all women—including Indigenous, rural, disabled, LGBTQIA+, and migrant women.

5. Role of Global Governance and Institutions

Global governance and institutions play a crucial role in advancing gender equality by shaping policies, enforcing legal frameworks, and promoting inclusive development. Organizations such as the United Nations (UN), World Bank, and OECD drive international efforts to eliminate gender disparities through policy advocacy, funding initiatives, and capacity-building programs. The Gender Equality and Governance Index (GEGI) highlights how governance structures influence gender equity, emphasizing the need for women's representation in leadership, education access, and economic participation. Additionally, the UNDP's gender equality programs focus on women's political empowerment, access to justice, and protection against gender-based violence, ensuring that governance systems uphold human rights. Institutions also play a vital role in peacekeeping and conflict resolution, as gender-inclusive approaches lead to more effective and sustainable peace efforts. Strengthening gender-responsive institutions through constitutional reforms, anti-discrimination laws, and gender budgeting enhances accountability and long-term progress.

International organizations, development agencies, and multilateral forums must advance inclusive growth by:

- Aligning national policies with SDG Goal 5 (Gender Equality) and Goal 10 (Reduced Inequalities).
- Enforcing international labor and human rights standards.
- Supporting South-South cooperation and knowledge exchange.
- Financing gender-responsive development through aid and debt relief.

6. Civil Society, Movements, and Social Innovation

Civil society, social movements, and social innovation play a crucial role in advancing gender equality and empowerment by driving systemic change and influencing policy decisions. Women-led civil society organizations (CSOs) and grassroots movements have historically been at the forefront of advocating for legal rights, economic inclusion, and social justice. These movements challenge discriminatory norms, amplify marginalized voices, and create sustainable solutions for gender-based inequalities.

Social movements such as #MeToo, Ni Una Menos, and the Women's March have reshaped public discourse on gender-based violence and workplace discrimination, leading to policy reforms and increased accountability. Additionally, organizations like UN Women's Fund for Gender Equality support national women-led CSOs, transforming funding into high-impact initiatives that benefit millions.

Social innovation further strengthens gender equality efforts by integrating technology, entrepreneurship, and community-driven solutions into empowerment strategies. Initiatives such as digital literacy programs, gender-responsive budgeting, and inclusive leadership training ensure that women have access to economic opportunities and decision-making platforms.

Grassroots activism and feminist movements are critical drivers of change. The future must empower:

- Women's organizations and community networks.
- Participatory models of governance and budgeting.
- Innovative financing (e.g., gender bonds, impact investing).
- Artistic and cultural platforms that reshape social norms.

7. Measuring Progress Toward Gender Justice

Measuring progress toward gender justice requires a combination of quantitative and qualitative indicators that assess equity, empowerment, and systemic change. Traditional development metrics often overlook gender-specific disparities, making gender-focused indices essential for tracking advancements. Key indicators include the Gender-related Development Index (GDI), which adjusts the Human Development Index (HDI) to reflect gender disparities in health, education, and income, and the Gender Empowerment Measure (GEM), which evaluates women's participation in economic and political spheres.

Effective monitoring frameworks, such as the European Institute for Gender Equality's Gender Equality Plan, emphasize SMART targets (Specific, Measurable, Attainable, Realistic, Time-bound) to ensure accountability and continuous improvement. Additionally, global initiatives like the United Nations Sustainable Development Goals (SDGs) integrate gender-specific indicators to measure progress across sectors.

Moving forward requires rigorous monitoring and evaluation. Indicators should go beyond numerical targets to assess:

- Empowerment, agency, and autonomy.
- Institutional transformation and power redistribution.

- Resilience, wellbeing, and life outcomes.

Integrated data systems must include sex-, age-, and location-disaggregated data and qualitative assessments.

8. Conclusion

The road to inclusive growth and gender justice is both a moral imperative and a strategic necessity. A future where all individuals, regardless of gender, can thrive demands bold, systemic, and collaborative action. By embedding gender justice into the core of economic, political, technological, and social systems, societies can achieve not only fairness but also resilience, innovation, and sustainability.

References

- *UN Women. (2023). Turning Promises into Action: Gender Equality in the 2030 Agenda.*
- *World Bank. (2022). Inclusive Growth and Gender Equality: Policy Frameworks.*
- *Oxfam. (2023). Rethinking Growth: Feminist Economics for a Just Transition.*
- *OECD. (2022). Gender Equality and the Future of Work.*
- *UNDP. (2023). Human Development Report: Gender Justice and Development.*

CHAPTER THIRTEEN

Women Entrepreneurs and the Gendered Business Ecosystem

Author: *Dr. Aaiman Siddiqui, Assistant Professor at Noida Institute of Engineering and Technology*
Co-Author: *Ms. Shruti Mittal, Assistant Professor at Noida Institute of Engineering and Technology*

Abstract

Entrepreneurship offers a powerful pathway for women's economic empowerment, autonomy, and leadership. Yet, women entrepreneurs often navigate a business ecosystem that is gendered in structure, access, and opportunity. This chapter explores the challenges and enablers for women-led enterprises, examining the structural barriers, institutional frameworks, and cultural norms that shape the entrepreneurial journey. It presents key policy recommendations, highlights emerging trends such as digital entrepreneurship and social enterprises, and calls for an inclusive, equitable business environment that fosters women's full participation in economic life.

1. Introduction

Women entrepreneurship is on the rise across the globe, driven by necessity, innovation, and the desire for self-determination. However, the environment in which women build and grow businesses is not neutral—it reflects broader gender disparities in access to capital, markets, mentorship, and decision-making. Addressing these gaps is essential for unlocking the full potential of women entrepreneurs and achieving inclusive economic growth.

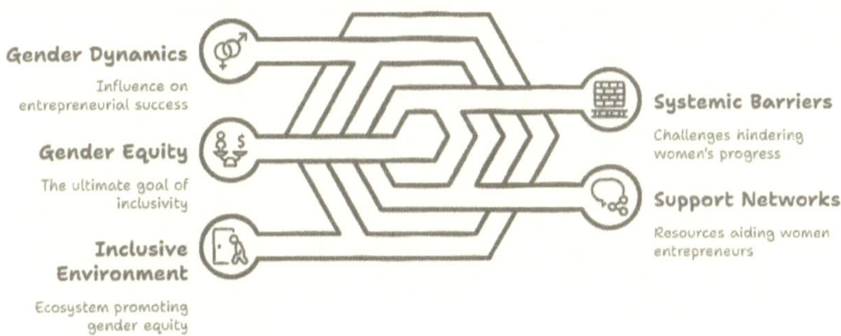

Gender Equity in Entrepreneurship

2. The Gendered Nature of Business Ecosystems

The gendered nature of business ecosystems highlights the structural inequalities that shape entrepreneurial opportunities for men and women. Research shows that women entrepreneurs face systemic barriers, including limited access to funding, mentorship, and market networks, which hinder their ability to scale businesses. Entrepreneurial ecosystems often reinforce gender biases, with male-dominated investment networks and policy frameworks favoring traditional business models. Studies indicate that women-led ventures receive significantly less venture capital funding compared to male-led businesses, despite demonstrating equal or higher profitability.

To create inclusive business ecosystems, experts advocate for gender-responsive policies, equitable access to financial resources, and mentorship programs that support women entrepreneurs. Initiatives such as gender lens investing and women-focused incubators aim to bridge these gaps, fostering a more balanced entrepreneurial landscape.

The business ecosystem encompasses a range of interconnected institutions, policies, services, and networks that support or hinder entrepreneurial activity. For women, this ecosystem is often shaped by:

- **Structural barriers,** such as lack of property rights, limited access to credit, and inadequate legal protection.
- **Sociocultural norms** that define gender roles and restrict women's mobility, time, or authority.
- **Discriminatory practices** in investment, procurement, and networking opportunities.
- **Underrepresentation** in business leadership, chambers of commerce, and trade associations.

These systemic challenges require targeted interventions at multiple levels—from grassroots programs to national policy reforms.

3. Global Trends in Women's Entrepreneurship

Global trends in women's entrepreneurship reveal significant shifts in startup activity, business ownership, and innovation. According to the Global Entrepreneurship Monitor (GEM) 2023/24 Women's Entrepreneurship Report, women's startup activity rates have risen from 6.1% (2001-2005) to 10.4% (2021-2023) across 30 GEM-participating countries. High-growth entrepreneurship among women is increasing, with one in three high-growth entrepreneurs being female. Younger women are driving entrepreneurship, particularly in low-income countries, where 28.2% of women express entrepreneurial ambitions. However, challenges persist, including limited access to funding, market networks, and mentorship, leading to higher business exit rates among female entrepreneurs. Countries like France, the Netherlands, and Hungary have seen women's startup rates more than double over the past two decades. Addressing structural barriers through gender-responsive policies, financial inclusion, and mentorship programs is crucial for fostering a more balanced entrepreneurial landscape.

Despite barriers, women entrepreneurs are transforming industries and communities worldwide. Key trends include:

- **Rise of women-led startups** in sectors such as fintech, healthtech, education, and fashion.
- **Growth of social enterprises,** often led by women to address community needs while generating income.
- **Increased digital entrepreneurship,** especially among younger and urban women using e-commerce and mobile platforms.

- **Expansion of women-focused incubators,** networks, and funding programs across regions.

Yet, disparities persist. According to the Global Entrepreneurship Monitor (2023), women are still 30% less likely than men to start a business in many regions, and their ventures often remain smaller and less profitable due to structural constraints.

4. Key Challenges Faced by Women Entrepreneurs

Women entrepreneurs face several key challenges that hinder their ability to start, sustain, and scale businesses. Access to funding remains a significant barrier, as women-led ventures receive disproportionately lower investment compared to male-led businesses. Gender bias in business networks further limits opportunities, with women often excluded from influential circles that provide mentorship and market access. Balancing personal and professional responsibilities is another challenge, as societal expectations frequently place a heavier burden on women to manage household duties alongside their entrepreneurial pursuits. Additionally, limited access to technology and digital platforms restricts growth, particularly in regions where digital literacy and infrastructure are lacking. Legal and regulatory barriers, including complex business registration processes and discriminatory policies, further complicate entrepreneurship for women. Addressing these challenges requires gender-responsive policies, financial inclusion initiatives, and mentorship programs that empower women to thrive in business.

a. Access to Finance

Access to finance remains a significant barrier for women entrepreneurs, limiting their ability to start, sustain, and scale businesses. Women-led ventures often face challenges such as restricted access to credit, lower investment rates, and gender biases in financial institutions. Studies indicate that women entrepreneurs receive less venture capital funding compared to their male counterparts, despite demonstrating equal or higher profitability. Initiatives like the Women Entrepreneurs Finance Initiative (We-Fi) aim to bridge this gap by scaling up access to financial products, expanding networks, and providing mentorship opportunities. Additionally, microfinance programs have proven effective in supporting women-owned businesses, ensuring financial inclusion and economic empowerment. Addressing these disparities requires gender-responsive financial policies, investor education, and targeted funding mechanisms to create a more equitable entrepreneurial landscape.

Women often lack the collateral or credit history required to obtain loans. Venture capital and private equity markets are even more exclusionary—less than 3% of global VC funding goes to women-led startups.

b. Education and Skills Gaps

Education and skills gaps remain significant barriers for women entrepreneurs, limiting their ability to compete in business ecosystems. Many women face challenges such as limited access to formal education, lack of mentorship, and insufficient technical training, which hinder their entrepreneurial success. Studies show that gender biases in education systems often discourage women from pursuing fields like STEM, finance, and business management, restricting their opportunities for high-growth ventures. Additionally, soft skills such as negotiation, leadership, and digital literacy are crucial for business success but are often underdeveloped due to societal norms and limited training programs. Initiatives like gender-responsive entrepreneurship education and vocational training aim to bridge these gaps by providing tailored learning experiences, mentorship programs, and access to business networks. Addressing these disparities requires policy interventions, corporate partnerships, and inclusive educational frameworks to ensure women have equal opportunities to thrive in entrepreneurship.

Many women have limited access to formal training in financial literacy, business planning, and technology. While informal knowledge networks exist, these may not be scalable or comprehensive.

c. Work-Life Balance and Time Poverty

Work-life balance and time poverty are significant challenges for women entrepreneurs, as they often juggle multiple responsibilities across professional and personal spheres. Many women face time constraints due to caregiving duties, household management, and business operations, leading to stress, burnout, and reduced productivity. Studies indicate that women entrepreneurs devote significantly more time to family responsibilities than their male counterparts, impacting their ability to scale businesses effectively.

Self-employment offers flexibility, but it does not eliminate the pressures of balancing work and life, especially in societies where traditional gender roles persist. Strategies such as delegation, structured time management, and supportive workplace policies can help mitigate these challenges. Additionally, government initiatives and corporate programs that promote affordable childcare, parental leave, and flexible work arrangements contribute to a more balanced entrepreneurial ecosystem.

Due to caregiving responsibilities and unpaid labor, women entrepreneurs face time constraints that affect their ability to network, travel, or scale their ventures.

d. Legal and Regulatory Barriers

Legal and regulatory barriers pose significant challenges for women entrepreneurs, often limiting their ability to start, sustain, and expand businesses. Many countries still have discriminatory laws that restrict women's access to credit, property ownership, and business registration, making it harder for them to secure financial independence. Complex bureaucratic processes and gender biases in legal frameworks further hinder women's participation in entrepreneurial ecosystems. For instance, some nations require spousal consent for business loans, while others impose restrictions on women's employment in certain industries. Additionally, limited access to legal support and resources exacerbates these challenges, leaving women entrepreneurs vulnerable to contract disputes, financial risks, and regulatory hurdles. Addressing these barriers requires gender-responsive legal reforms, digitalization of business registration processes, and targeted policy interventions to create a more equitable business environment.

In many countries, laws still restrict women's ability to sign contracts, own land, or register a business without a male guardian or spouse.

e. Bias in Investment and Mentorship

Bias in investment and mentorship significantly impacts women entrepreneurs, limiting their access to funding and professional guidance. Research indicates that male investors and mentors are more likely to support male entrepreneurs, creating barriers for women seeking financial backing and industry connections. This bias is often unconscious, stemming from traditional business networks that favor established male-led ventures.

Women entrepreneurs frequently receive lower venture capital funding compared to their male counterparts, despite demonstrating equal or higher profitability. Additionally, mentorship networks tend to be gender-segregated, with male mentors disproportionately favoring male mentees, making it harder for women to access critical business insights and opportunities.

To address these challenges, initiatives such as gender lens investing, women-focused incubators, and mentorship programs aim to create more equitable entrepreneurial ecosystems. Increasing female representation in investment and mentorship roles is a crucial step toward mitigating these biases and fostering inclusive business environments.

Women are underrepresented in investor networks, and gender bias often leads to skepticism about their leadership or business models, particularly in male-dominated industries.

5. Strategies and Policy Interventions

Effective strategies and policy interventions are crucial for advancing women's entrepreneurship and addressing systemic barriers. Key strategies include improving access to capital, expanding mentorship networks, and creating inclusive regulatory frameworks. Governments and organizations worldwide are implementing gender-responsive policies to support women entrepreneurs, such as targeted financial programs, skill development initiatives, and digital literacy training.

For instance, the Women Entrepreneurs Finance Initiative (We-Fi) focuses on scaling up financial access and expanding business networks for women-led enterprises. Additionally, microfinance programs and government-backed credit schemes help bridge funding gaps, ensuring financial inclusion. Expanding mentorship and networking opportunities is another critical intervention, as women often face limited access to industry connections and business guidance.

Policy frameworks that challenge cultural biases, promote equal pay, and streamline business registration processes contribute to a more equitable entrepreneurial landscape. Countries like India and France have introduced women-focused incubators and investment incentives, fostering innovation and business growth.

a. Financial Inclusion and Gender-Responsive Lending

Financial inclusion and gender-responsive lending are essential for bridging economic disparities and ensuring that women have equitable access to financial resources. Despite progress, women entrepreneurs still face systemic barriers, including limited access to credit, restrictive collateral requirements, and gender biases in financial institutions. Studies indicate that women-led businesses receive significantly less venture capital funding, despite demonstrating higher repayment rates and profitability compared to male-led ventures.

To address these challenges, financial institutions are adopting gender-fair lending portfolios, integrating bias-free credit assessments, tailored financial products, and digital financial inclusion strategies. Initiatives such as microfinance programs, gender-responsive banking policies, and fintech solutions are helping women entrepreneurs overcome financial barriers and expand their businesses. Additionally, digital financial services (DFS) are playing a crucial role in enhancing financial accessibility, particularly for women in underserved regions.

Would you like insights on specific financial inclusion strategies or case studies? You can explore more details here and here.

- Microfinance, blended finance, and gender-lens investing can improve access to capital.
- Credit guarantee schemes and collateral-free loans tailored for women can bridge funding gaps.

b. Capacity Building and Mentorship

Capacity building and mentorship are essential for empowering women entrepreneurs, equipping them with the skills, knowledge, and networks needed to succeed. Programs like WING – Women Rise Together in India provide structured mentorship, business training, and incubation opportunities to support aspiring and established women entrepreneurs. Similarly, initiatives such as Advancing Women Entrepreneurs (AWE-India Network) focus on bridging gaps in education, access to finance, and socio-cultural barriers through mentorship and policy advocacy.

Governments and organizations worldwide are investing in capacity-building workshops, leadership training, and peer networking to enhance women's entrepreneurial capabilities. These efforts not only foster business growth but also create inclusive ecosystems where women can thrive.

- Business incubation programs specifically for women can provide mentorship, technical assistance, and networking.
- Public-private partnerships can facilitate scalable training in digital skills and business management.

c. Regulatory Reform

Regulatory reform plays a crucial role in removing barriers that hinder women entrepreneurs from accessing financial resources, market opportunities, and legal protections. Many existing regulations disproportionately affect women, such as complex business registration processes, restrictive property laws, and gender biases in financial institutions. Reforming these frameworks ensures equitable access to credit, streamlined licensing procedures, and gender-responsive taxation policies, fostering a more inclusive business environment.

Governments worldwide are implementing gender-sensitive regulatory policies, such as simplified business registration for women-led enterprises, affirmative procurement policies, and legal protections against workplace discrimination. Initiatives like India's Women Entrepreneurship Platform (WEP) and OECD's gender-responsive entrepreneurship policies aim to enhance financial inclusion, reduce bureaucratic hurdles, and promote equitable business ecosystems.

- Eliminate legal barriers that inhibit women's economic agency.
- Simplify business registration and taxation procedures for small women-led businesses.

d. Inclusive Procurement

Inclusive procurement is a strategic approach that integrates gender considerations into procurement policies, ensuring that women-owned businesses have equitable access to supply chains and market opportunities. Despite women owning one-third of registered SMEs globally, large corporations and governments allocate less than 1% of their procurement budgets to women-led enterprises.

To address this disparity, initiatives like Gender-Responsive Procurement (GRP) embed equity-driven policies into corporate and government purchasing decisions, fostering economic empowerment for women entrepreneurs. Programs such as Sourcing2Equal, led by the International Finance Corporation (IFC), aim to connect thousands of women entrepreneurs to corporate procurement opportunities, helping them overcome structural barriers like limited access to finance and business networks.

Governments are also implementing public procurement mandates, such as India's Public Procurement Policy for MSEs, which requires 3% of annual procurement to be sourced from women-owned businesses. However, actual procurement figures remain below target, highlighting the need for stronger enforcement and capacity-building initiatives.

- Governments and corporations can adopt supplier diversity policies that include quotas for women-owned businesses.
- Transparent procurement processes ensure fair competition and access to larger markets.

e. Social Norms and Awareness

Social norms and awareness play a crucial role in shaping gender equality, influencing behaviors, attitudes, and institutional structures. Many gender disparities stem from deeply ingrained societal norms that dictate roles, expectations, and opportunities for men and women. Raising awareness about these biases is essential for fostering inclusive environments and driving systemic change. Initiatives such as gender-sensitive education, media representation, and community engagement programs help challenge stereotypes and promote equitable perspectives. Organizations like UN Women and the European Institute for Gender Equality (EIGE) emphasize the importance of awareness campaigns, policy advocacy, and behavioral change strategies to dismantle discriminatory norms. Studies show that societies with strong gender awareness frameworks experience higher levels of economic participation, improved social cohesion, and reduced gender-based violence.

- Media and education campaigns can challenge stereotypes and showcase successful women entrepreneurs as role models.
- Engage men and communities in supporting women's business endeavors.

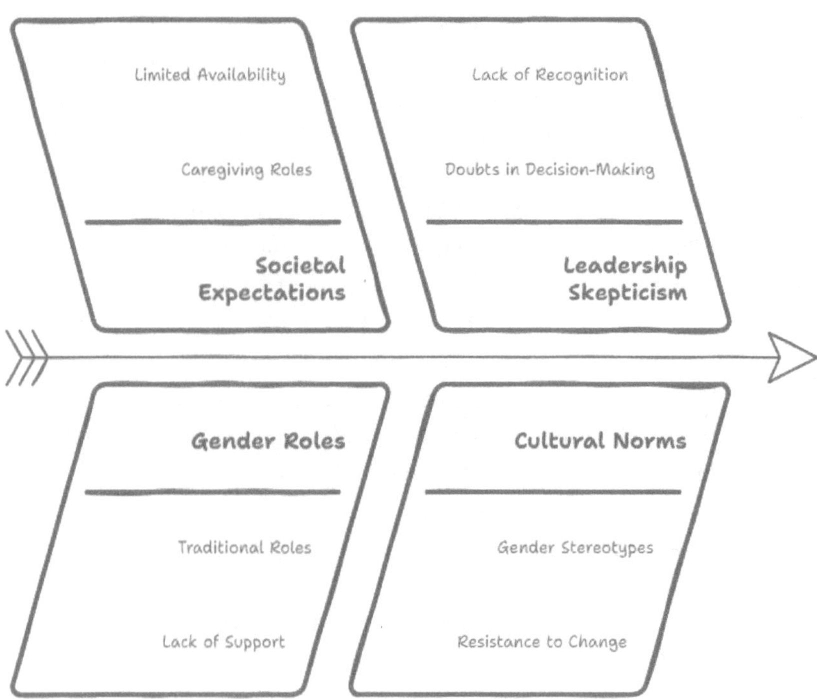

Challenges to Women's Entrepreneurial Ambitions

6. Case Examples of Successful Interventions

Several successful interventions have empowered women entrepreneurs by addressing financial barriers, mentorship gaps, and policy constraints. For instance, the Women's Business Ownership Act (USA) led to the creation of Women's Business Centers, providing financial assistance and training programs for female entrepreneurs. In India, the Self Employed Women's Association (SEWA) has been instrumental in supporting women in the informal sector through microfinance and skill development initiatives.

Another notable example is Kinara Capital (India), which offers collateral-free loans to women-led businesses, helping them scale operations and improve financial stability. In the UK, Revenge Capital focuses on funding women entrepreneurs in male-dominated industries, ensuring equitable access to investment opportunities.

Additionally, India's Public Procurement Policy for MSEs mandates that 3% of annual procurement be sourced from women-owned businesses, fostering economic inclusion. However, challenges remain in credit accessibility, regulatory hurdles, and mentorship networks, highlighting the need for stronger enforcement and capacity-building initiatives.

- **SheTrades (International Trade Centre)** connects women entrepreneurs to global markets and offers training on export readiness.
- **Goldman Sachs 10,000 Women Program** provides business education and access to capital for women in emerging economies.
- **WEConnect International** certifies women-owned businesses and connects them with global supply chains.
- **India's MUDRA Scheme** offers microloans to non-corporate, non-farm small/micro enterprises, with special emphasis on women beneficiaries.

7. The Future of Women's Entrepreneurship

The future of women's entrepreneurship is poised for significant growth, driven by technological advancements, policy support, and evolving business ecosystems. Studies indicate that women-led businesses are expanding rapidly, contributing to innovation, job creation, and economic resilience. Emerging trends suggest that digital platforms, gender-responsive financing, and inclusive leadership models will shape the entrepreneurial landscape in the coming years.

Key developments include increased access to venture capital for women entrepreneurs, the rise of women-focused incubators and accelerators, and the integration of AI-driven business solutions to enhance efficiency. Additionally, social and cultural shifts are fostering more equitable business environments, with governments and organizations implementing gender-inclusive policies to support women in entrepreneurship.

The future lies in a gender-intentional ecosystem that not only removes barriers but actively builds platforms for women's entrepreneurial success. Emerging opportunities include:

- **Green and circular economy enterprises,** where women can lead sustainability initiatives.
- **Tech-enabled small businesses,** including AI, blockchain, and mobile commerce.
- **Diaspora and cross-border women networks** that facilitate global partnerships and innovation.

Digital platforms, inclusive policies, and women-led investment funds will play a key role in enabling transformative entrepreneurship.

8. Conclusion

Women entrepreneurs are vital agents of economic and social change. However, to fully unleash their potential, we must reimagine and reconstruct the business ecosystem to be truly inclusive. This requires systemic policy changes, cultural shifts, and targeted investments. When empowered with equal opportunities, women entrepreneurs not only build successful businesses but also create jobs, uplift communities, and contribute to more resilient and equitable economies.

References

- *Global Entrepreneurship Monitor (GEM). (2023). Women's Entrepreneurship Report.*
- *World Bank. (2022). Women, Business and the Law.*
- *UN Women. (2023). Financing Women's Economic Empowerment.*
- *ITC SheTrades. (2023). Women in Trade: Access and Empowerment.*
- *WEConnect International. (2022). Global Impact Report.*

CHAPTER FOURTEEN

Climate Change, Environmental Justice, and Women's Leadership

Author: Ms. Shashi Bala, Assistant Professor at Greater Noida Institute of Technology, Greater Noida

Abstract

Climate change is not gender-neutral. Women—particularly those in marginalized and resource-poor communities—are disproportionately affected by environmental degradation and climate-related disasters. Yet, women are not only victims of climate injustice; they are also powerful agents of environmental change. This chapter explores the nexus between gender, environmental justice, and climate action. It emphasizes women's leadership in climate governance, grassroots sustainability initiatives, and global environmental policy. It also discusses the importance of gender-responsive climate strategies and highlights pathways for inclusive and sustainable environmental futures.

1. Introduction

The climate crisis poses one of the greatest global threats of our time, with far-reaching consequences for ecosystems, economies, and human wellbeing. However, the impacts of climate change are unevenly distributed. Women—especially in the Global South—face greater exposure to climate hazards due to their roles in agriculture, caregiving, and natural resource management. At the same time, their leadership in adaptation, conservation, and resilience-building is often overlooked or underutilized in policy and practice.

Where Women's Leadership Drives Climate Justice

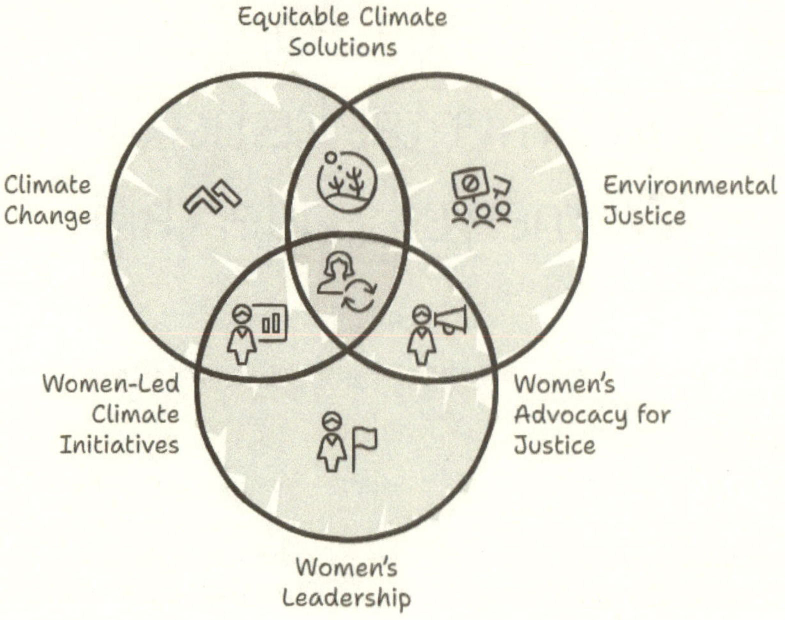

Where Women's Leadership Drives Climate Justice

2. Climate Vulnerabilities Through a Gender Lens

Climate vulnerabilities disproportionately affect women and marginalized communities, making gender-responsive climate policies essential for equitable adaptation and resilience. Studies indicate that women are more likely to experience economic and social hardships due to climate change, as they often bear the responsibility for securing food, water, and energy resources. The climate crisis is not gender-neutral, with women facing higher health risks, displacement, and economic instability compared to men.

Gender inequalities, fueled by societal norms and limited access to resources, exacerbate climate-induced vulnerabilities. For instance, in rural areas, women's dependence on agriculture and natural resources makes them more susceptible to environmental degradation and extreme weather events. Additionally, climate-related disasters increase gender-based violence, as displacement and resource scarcity heighten social tensions.

To address these disparities, gender-responsive climate policies focus on inclusive decision-making, equitable resource distribution, and targeted adaptation strategies. Governments and organizations are integrating women's leadership in climate governance, ensuring that sustainability efforts reflect diverse needs.

Women are disproportionately affected by climate change due to:

- **Poverty and economic marginalization,** which reduce access to adaptive resources.
- **Dependence on natural resources** for livelihoods, particularly in agriculture and water collection.
- **Sociocultural norms** that limit mobility, decision-making power, and access to information.
- **Health impacts,** including increased vulnerability during pregnancy and childbirth in disaster settings.

For example, during extreme weather events such as floods or cyclones, women and girls are more likely to be displaced, suffer violence, or lose access to education and health services.

3. Environmental Justice and Gender Equity

Environmental justice and gender equity are deeply interconnected, as women and marginalized communities often bear the brunt of environmental degradation and climate change. The triple planetary crisis—climate change, pollution, and biodiversity loss—disproportionately affects women, particularly those in rural areas and crisis-affected regions. Limited access to land, natural resources, and environmental decision-making further exacerbates gender inequalities in climate resilience.

Gender-responsive environmental policies focus on equitable resource distribution, legal protections, and inclusive governance, ensuring that women can actively participate in sustainability efforts. Studies indicate that integrating women's leadership in climate governance enhances policy effectiveness and fosters community-driven solutions. Organizations like UNDP and UN Women advocate for gender-sensitive environmental frameworks, emphasizing the need for justice, accountability, and environmental rights.

Environmental justice addresses the fair treatment and meaningful involvement of all people—regardless of gender, race, or income—in environmental policy and action. A gender-equitable approach to environmental justice recognizes that:

- Women's environmental burdens are shaped by social, political, and economic inequalities.
- Policies must include women in design and implementation, not only as beneficiaries but as decision-makers.
- Indigenous and rural women are custodians of traditional ecological knowledge critical for conservation.

Ignoring gender perspectives in climate action can deepen existing inequalities and undermine sustainability outcomes.

4. Women as Environmental Leaders and Change Agents

Women play a crucial role as environmental leaders and change agents, driving sustainability efforts and advocating for climate justice. Despite facing systemic barriers, women have been at the forefront of community-driven conservation, policy advocacy, and corporate sustainability initiatives. Studies show that countries with higher female representation in governance are more likely to adopt stronger environmental policies and ratify climate agreements.

Women-led grassroots movements have pioneered climate adaptation strategies, integrating traditional ecological knowledge with modern sustainability practices. Organizations such as UN Women and the European Investment Bank emphasize the importance of women's leadership in climate governance, highlighting their ability to prioritize long-term environmental solutions. Additionally, female executives in corporate sectors are driving ethical governance, sustainable business models, and green innovation, proving that profitability and sustainability can coexist.

Components of Environmental Justice

Components of Environmental Justice

Despite structural barriers, women around the world are leading innovative and transformative environmental initiatives:

a. Grassroots Environmental Movements

Grassroots environmental movements play a vital role in advancing gender equality and environmental justice, as they empower local communities—especially women—to lead sustainability efforts. Women have historically been at the forefront of environmental activism, advocating for land rights, climate resilience, and ecological conservation. Movements such as the Chipko Movement in India, where women protected forests from deforestation, and Kenya's Green Belt Movement, founded by Wangari Maathai to promote reforestation and women's empowerment, exemplify the intersection of gender and environmental activism.

These movements challenge corporate exploitation, unsustainable development, and environmental degradation, ensuring that marginalized voices are heard in climate governance. Studies highlight that women-led grassroots initiatives often prioritize community-driven solutions, sustainable agriculture, and climate adaptation strategies, making them essential for long-term environmental resilience.

- In India, the Chipko Movement saw rural women protect forests through non-violent resistance.
- In Kenya, Wangari Maathai's Green Belt Movement mobilized women to plant millions of trees, linking reforestation to women's empowerment.

b. Sustainable Agriculture and Food Security

Sustainable agriculture and food security are deeply intertwined with gender equality, as women play a crucial role in food production, yet often face systemic barriers in accessing resources, land, and financial support. Women make up 38% of agricultural employment globally, yet they experience higher food insecurity rates compared to men due to limited access to technology, markets, and decision-making platforms.

Gender-responsive agricultural policies focus on equitable land rights, financial inclusion, and access to sustainable farming techniques, ensuring that women farmers can contribute effectively to food security. Studies indicate that if women had the same level of access to agricultural resources as men, global food production could increase by 20-30%, significantly reducing hunger.

Additionally, initiatives such as climate-resilient farming, agroecology, and women-led cooperatives are transforming food systems, promoting sustainability while addressing gender disparities.

- Women farmers are leading agroecology and permaculture movements that build climate resilience.
- Female-led cooperatives are restoring degraded lands and promoting organic farming.

c. Climate Advocacy and Global Governance

Climate advocacy and global governance are essential for advancing gender equality and ensuring that women's voices are included in climate decision-making. Women-led climate movements and organizations play a crucial role in shaping policies, influencing international agreements, and driving sustainable solutions.

Recent discussions at CSW69 highlighted the intersection of gender, climate, and conflict, emphasizing the need for feminist crisis responses that address the gendered impacts of climate change. Additionally, the Women & Gender Constituency at COP29 continues to advocate for gender-just climate solutions, ensuring that global climate policies integrate gender perspectives.

Governments and international bodies are increasingly recognizing the importance of gender-responsive climate governance, with initiatives such as the UNDP's framework for integrating gender equality into national climate plans. These efforts aim to enhance women's leadership in climate negotiations, improve access to climate finance, and promote inclusive environmental policies.

Would you like insights on specific gender-responsive climate policies or case studies? You can explore more details here.

- Women leaders such as Christiana Figueres (former UNFCCC Executive Secretary) and Greta Thunberg have played pivotal roles in shaping global climate discourse.
- Gender-just climate policies are increasingly championed by women in parliaments, municipalities, and international forums.

5. Gender-Responsive Climate Policy and Planning

Gender-responsive climate policy and planning ensure that climate action considers the unique vulnerabilities and contributions of women and marginalized communities. Studies indicate that women are disproportionately affected by climate change, facing higher risks of displacement, food insecurity, and economic instability. Integrating gender perspectives into climate policies enhances adaptation strategies, resource allocation, and decision-making processes, leading to more equitable and effective solutions.

Recent global efforts, such as the Enhanced Lima Work Programme on Gender and Climate Change, emphasize the importance of gender mainstreaming in climate governance. Countries are now incorporating gender-responsive frameworks into their Nationally Determined Contributions (NDCs) under the Paris Agreement, ensuring that climate policies address gender disparities. Additionally, initiatives like WinWASH's climate-resilient WASH programs highlight the need for inclusive infrastructure planning, ensuring that women's voices shape sustainable development.

For climate action to be effective and equitable, it must be gender-responsive. Key strategies include:

- **Gender mainstreaming** in Nationally Determined Contributions (NDCs) under the Paris Agreement.
- **Targeted climate finance** for women-led mitigation and adaptation projects.
- **Capacity-building** programs to enhance women's participation in climate science and governance.
- **Inclusive disaster preparedness** and response planning that addresses gender-specific vulnerabilities.

Integrating gender analysis into climate policies ensures that interventions are fair, inclusive, and sustainable.

6. Case Studies of Women's Environmental Leadership

Gender-responsive climate policy and planning ensure that climate action considers the unique vulnerabilities and contributions of women and marginalized communities. Studies indicate that women are disproportionately affected by climate change, facing higher risks of displacement, food insecurity, and economic instability. Integrating gender perspectives into climate policies enhances adaptation strategies, resource allocation, and decision-making processes, leading to more equitable and effective solutions. Recent global efforts, such as the Enhanced Lima Work Programme on Gender and Climate Change, emphasize the importance of gender mainstreaming in climate governance. Countries are now incorporating gender-responsive frameworks into their Nationally Determined Contributions (NDCs) under the Paris Agreement, ensuring that climate policies address gender disparities. Additionally, initiatives like WinWASH's climate-resilient WASH programs highlight the need for inclusive infrastructure planning, ensuring that women's voices shape sustainable development.

- **Nepal:** Women's Forest User Groups manage over 30% of community forests, reducing deforestation and improving livelihoods.
- **Ethiopia:** Women in Tigray have developed water harvesting and climate-smart agriculture techniques to combat drought.

- **Pacific Islands:** Women-led NGOs are leading coastal resilience programs that incorporate Indigenous knowledge and gender-sensitive approaches.

These cases demonstrate that investing in women's environmental leadership yields benefits for communities, biodiversity, and climate resilience.

7. Barriers to Women's Full Participation

Women face numerous barriers to full participation in economic, social, and political spheres, limiting their opportunities for growth and leadership. Systemic discrimination remains a significant challenge, with institutional policies often reinforcing gender inequalities. Social norms and cultural practices further restrict women's mobility, decision-making power, and access to education and employment. Gender stereotypes perpetuate biases that discourage women from pursuing leadership roles or entering male-dominated industries. Economic inequality is another major hurdle, as women frequently earn less than men for the same work and have limited access to financial resources. Lack of gender representation in governance and corporate leadership exacerbates these disparities, reducing women's influence in policy-making and business decisions. Additionally, gender-based violence, digital exclusion, and restricted access to healthcare and education further hinder women's ability to participate fully in society. Addressing these barriers requires comprehensive policy reforms, gender-sensitive education, and inclusive economic strategies to create equitable opportunities for all.

While progress has been made, women still face barriers in environmental leadership:

- **Underrepresentation** in climate negotiation delegations and high-level decision-making.
- **Limited access** to land, credit, and technology.
- **Patriarchal norms** that devalue women's contributions and leadership.
- **Inadequate data** disaggregated by gender in environmental assessments.

Overcoming these barriers requires systemic change in education, governance, financing, and cultural narratives.

8. Pathways for Inclusive Environmental Futures

Pathways for inclusive environmental futures emphasize equity, sustainability, and gender-responsive policies to ensure that marginalized communities, particularly women, actively participate in climate governance and environmental decision-making. Studies indicate that women and vulnerable groups disproportionately experience climate-related challenges, including displacement, food insecurity, and resource scarcity. Addressing these disparities requires inclusive frameworks that integrate gender-sensitive climate policies, equitable access to green technologies, and community-driven conservation efforts.

Global initiatives such as UN Women's Gender Equality and Sustainable Development Pathways Approach advocate for intersectional strategies that align environmental sustainability with gender equity. Additionally, just transition policies focus on ensuring women's access to green economic opportunities, leadership roles, and climate finance, fostering long-term resilience.

Would you like insights on specific gender-responsive environmental policies or case studies? You can explore more details here and here.

To advance gender justice and climate resilience, the following strategies are essential:

- **Inclusive climate governance structures** that prioritize gender balance and intersectional representation.
- **Support for women's environmental entrepreneurship** in sectors like renewable energy and waste management.
- **Gender-responsive education and green skills training,** especially for youth and marginalized women.
- **Global alliances** that fund, recognize, and scale women-led climate innovations.

A feminist approach to climate action not only addresses inequities but also enhances the effectiveness and legitimacy of environmental policy.

9. Conclusion

Climate change is a profound gender issue, demanding inclusive, justice-oriented responses. Women are not passive victims but powerful leaders, innovators, and stewards of the Earth. Recognizing and investing in their knowledge, leadership, and agency is key to securing a sustainable and equitable future for all. True environmental justice cannot be achieved without gender justice.

References

- *UN Women. (2023). Gender Equality and Climate Change: A Feminist Roadmap.*
- *UNEP. (2022). Women and the Environment: Policy and Action Review.*
- *FAO. (2023). Gender and Climate-Resilient Agriculture.*
- *World Bank. (2022). Climate-Smart Development and Women's Empowerment.*
- *IPCC. (2023). Special Report on Climate Change and Gender Dimensions.*

CHAPTER FIFTEEN

Inclusive Innovation: Designing for and with Women

Author: Dr. Jitendra Singh, President ofVibrant Association for Scholarly Techniques, Upgrading, and Development of Yearners, Ghaziabad, Uttar Pradesh

Abstract

Innovation is a powerful force in driving economic growth, social transformation, and human development. However, when innovation systems exclude or marginalize women, they risk perpetuating existing inequalities and overlooking significant opportunities for inclusive progress. This chapter explores the concept of inclusive innovation, focusing on gender-responsive design and women's participation in innovation ecosystems. It highlights barriers that inhibit women's involvement in innovation and presents frameworks, examples, and strategies for ensuring that women are not just passive beneficiaries but active co-creators in the innovation process.

1. Introduction

Innovation has traditionally been framed as a neutral process driven by market needs and technological advancement. Yet, innovation is often embedded with biases—especially gender biases—that influence who designs, who benefits, and who is left behind. Inclusive innovation seeks to bridge this gap by ensuring that marginalized populations, including women, are meaningfully included in innovation systems, not only as users but also as designers, decision-makers, and entrepreneurs.

Designing for and with women is not just an ethical imperative but a strategic one. Innovations that are co-developed with women are more likely to be sustainable, equitable, and contextually appropriate.

2. Defining Inclusive Innovation

Inclusive innovation refers to the development of new ideas, products, and services that enhance social and economic well-being for marginalized or underserved communities. It aims to ensure that innovation is accessible, equitable, and beneficial to all, particularly those excluded from mainstream development. This approach integrates social, environmental, and economic considerations, fostering solutions that address systemic inequalities.

Studies highlight that inclusive innovation is not just about technology-driven advancements but also encompasses low-tech and social innovations that empower communities. It involves collaborative problem-solving, where those affected by challenges actively participate in designing solutions. Governments, businesses, and civil society organizations are increasingly adopting inclusive innovation frameworks to drive sustainable development and economic empowerment.

Inclusive innovation refers to the creation and application of knowledge, technologies, and services that address the needs of underserved populations. When applied through a gender lens, it involves:

- **Co-creation with women** to ensure relevance and usability.
- **Access and affordability** of innovations for diverse women across socioeconomic and geographic spectrums.
- **Empowerment and capacity-building** to enable women to innovate and lead.
- **Systemic change** in institutional and policy structures that exclude or ignore women's perspectives.

Inclusive innovation recognizes diversity within women themselves—accounting for factors like age, disability, ethnicity, location, and income.

3. Barriers to Women's Participation in Innovation Systems

Women face significant barriers to full participation in innovation systems, limiting their ability to contribute to technological advancements and entrepreneurial growth. Gender biases in STEM fields often discourage women from pursuing careers in science, technology, engineering, and mathematics, leading to underrepresentation in research and leadership roles. Limited access to funding and investment further restricts women-led startups, as venture capital firms tend to favor male entrepreneurs. Additionally, workplace discrimination and lack of mentorship create obstacles for women seeking career progression in innovation-driven industries.

Studies indicate that women in STEM leadership roles remain disproportionately low, despite evidence that diverse teams drive higher innovation and financial performance. In India, women hold only 14% of leadership positions in STEM, highlighting the need for inclusive policies and mentorship programs. Addressing these barriers requires gender-responsive funding mechanisms, equitable hiring practices, and supportive workplace cultures to foster a more inclusive innovation ecosystem.

a. Gender Bias in Research and Development

Gender bias in research and development remains a significant challenge, influencing everything from funding allocation to study design and data interpretation. Studies indicate that historical biases in scientific research have led to underrepresentation of women in clinical trials, technology development, and STEM leadership roles. This bias often results in medical treatments, AI algorithms, and workplace policies that fail to account for gender-specific differences, reinforcing systemic inequalities.

One major issue is androcentrism, where research predominantly focuses on male subjects, leading to misdiagnoses and ineffective treatments for women in fields like healthcare and pharmacology. Additionally, gender stereotypes in innovation ecosystems discourage women from pursuing leadership roles in R&D, limiting their contributions to technological advancements. Addressing these disparities requires gender-sensitive research methodologies, equitable funding distribution, and inclusive innovation policies to ensure diverse perspectives shape scientific progress.

Many R&D teams lack gender diversity, leading to blind spots in product design and service delivery. For example, early voice recognition systems failed to recognize female voices accurately due to male-dominated training datasets.

b. Limited Access to Resources

Limited access to resources remains a significant barrier for women entrepreneurs, affecting their ability to scale businesses and compete in the market. Women often face challenges in securing financial support, mentorship, technology, and market linkages, which are crucial for business growth. Studies indicate that women-led businesses receive disproportionately lower funding compared to male-led ventures, despite demonstrating equal or higher profitability. Additionally, restricted access to professional networks and industry insights limits opportunities for collaboration and expansion.

To address these disparities, initiatives such as Women Entrepreneurship Platform (WEP) in India provide mentorship, funding opportunities, and business development services to support women entrepreneurs. Government schemes like Mudra Yojana and Stand-Up India aim to bridge financial gaps by offering collateral-free loans and credit support. However, challenges persist in digital literacy, access to technology, and policy implementation, highlighting the need for stronger institutional support and inclusive economic frameworks.

Women often face constraints in accessing financial capital, technology, intellectual property rights, and education—resources that are foundational for participation in innovation ecosystems.

c. Cultural and Institutional Norms

Cultural and institutional norms significantly shape women's participation in entrepreneurship, often creating barriers that limit their access to resources, networks, and leadership opportunities. Societal expectations regarding gender roles frequently discourage women from pursuing business ventures, reinforcing stereotypes that associate entrepreneurship with male leadership. Institutional biases, such as restrictive policies on business ownership and financial access, further hinder women's ability to establish and scale enterprises.

In many regions, women entrepreneurs face challenges in securing funding due to ingrained biases in investment decisions, where male-led businesses are often prioritized. Additionally, workplace cultures that lack gender-inclusive policies contribute to disparities in mentorship and professional advancement. Addressing these issues requires policy reforms, gender-sensitive business regulations, and cultural shifts that promote equitable opportunities for women in entrepreneurship.

Social norms and stereotypes that discourage girls from studying STEM (science, technology, engineering, and mathematics) fields limit the talent pipeline for female innovators.

d. Exclusion from Policy and Innovation Networks

Women entrepreneurs often face exclusion from policy and innovation networks, limiting their ability to access funding, mentorship, and market opportunities. Studies indicate that institutional biases and gender stereotypes contribute to this exclusion, as many investment and policy decisions are made within male-dominated networks. Women-led businesses frequently struggle to secure venture capital, with investors often perceiving them as higher risk despite evidence of strong financial performance.

Additionally, policy frameworks in many countries fail to integrate gender-responsive measures, making it harder for women entrepreneurs to benefit from government support, tax incentives, and business development programs. The lack of women's representation in decision-making bodies further exacerbates these challenges, as policies often overlook the unique barriers faced by female entrepreneurs.

To address these disparities, initiatives such as gender-inclusive investment funds, women-focused incubators, and policy advocacy groups aim to create equitable access to innovation ecosystems. Governments and organizations are increasingly recognizing the need for inclusive entrepreneurship policies to foster diversity and economic growth.

Women are underrepresented in innovation policy dialogues, tech hubs, incubators, and patenting systems.

4. Principles of Designing for and with Women

Designing for and with women requires a gender-responsive approach that prioritizes equity, inclusivity, and accessibility throughout the innovation lifecycle. The Gender Innovation Principles, developed by UN Women, set a benchmark for integrating women into design, implementation, evaluation, scaling, and sustainability. These principles emphasize co-creation, ensuring that women actively participate in shaping solutions that address their unique needs.

Additionally, gender-inclusive design extends beyond products and services to urban planning and public spaces. Studies highlight that historical biases in urban design have led to exclusionary environments, limiting women's mobility and economic opportunities. Organizations like Kounkuey Design Initiative (KDI) advocate for community-led planning, ensuring that public spaces are safe, accessible, and equitable for all.

a. Participatory Design

Participatory design is an approach that actively involves stakeholders—especially marginalized groups—in the creation of solutions that address their needs. In the context of gender equality, participatory design ensures that women and underrepresented communities have a voice in shaping policies, technologies, and social initiatives. This method fosters collaborative problem-solving, where diverse perspectives contribute to more inclusive and effective outcomes.

Studies highlight that participatory design enhances equity, accessibility, and sustainability, particularly in gender-responsive innovation. Frameworks such as co-creation models and gender-sensitive participatory approaches integrate community insights into decision-making processes, ensuring that solutions reflect real-world challenges. Organizations like SUPERA and ICIMOD advocate for participatory methodologies in gender equality planning, emphasizing the importance of stakeholder engagement and inclusive governance.

Engaging women from diverse backgrounds in all stages of innovation—from ideation to testing—ensures that solutions reflect their realities and needs.

b. Context Sensitivity

Context sensitivity in gender equality refers to the ability to recognize and adapt to cultural, social, and institutional factors that shape gender dynamics. It involves understanding how historical biases, societal norms, and economic structures influence gender disparities and tailoring interventions accordingly. Studies highlight that gender-sensitive policies must be locally relevant, ensuring that solutions align with community needs, traditions, and systemic challenges.

For instance, gender-sensitive education frameworks help challenge stereotypes while respecting cultural contexts, fostering inclusive learning environments. Similarly, workplace policies that account for regional gender norms can enhance equity and representation without imposing rigid, one-size-fits-all solutions. Organizations like UNESCO and UNDP advocate for context-sensitive gender strategies, ensuring that interventions are effective, sustainable, and culturally appropriate.

Recognizing that women's challenges and opportunities differ across cultures, sectors, and life stages. For example, innovations for rural women should address mobility, literacy, and infrastructure constraints.

c. Affordability and Accessibility

Affordability and accessibility are crucial factors in achieving gender equality, ensuring that women and marginalized communities have equitable access to essential services, technology, and economic opportunities. Studies indicate that women face disproportionate barriers in accessing transport, healthcare, education, and digital technologies, often due to high costs, limited infrastructure, and societal norms. For instance, in many regions, public transport affordability and safety significantly impact women's mobility and economic participation. Similarly, digital access gaps persist, with women in low-income countries having less access to the internet and mobile technologies compared to men.

To address these disparities, governments and organizations are implementing gender-responsive policies, such as subsidized transport programs, affordable healthcare initiatives, and digital inclusion strategies. The Availability, Accessibility, Acceptability, and Quality (AAAQ) framework is widely used to identify barriers and improve service delivery for women in humanitarian settings.

Designing products and services that are financially accessible and usable by women with varying levels of education, connectivity, and digital literacy.

d. Scalability and Sustainability

Scalability and sustainability are crucial for advancing gender equality in innovation and entrepreneurship. Scalability ensures that gender-responsive initiatives can expand their impact, reaching more women and marginalized communities. This requires strong institutional support, adaptable frameworks, and inclusive funding mechanisms to sustain growth. Sustainability, on the other hand, focuses on long-term viability, ensuring that gender-inclusive policies and programs remain effective beyond initial implementation.

Organizations like ISEAL Alliance advocate for credible sustainability systems that integrate gender equality into business standards, environmental policies, and economic frameworks. Additionally, gender-transformative programs emphasize systemic change, ensuring that interventions are multiplicative, scalable, and sustainable. The UN Women Pathways Approach highlights the need for intersectional strategies that align gender equality with sustainable development.

Inclusive innovations should be designed for long-term impact and wide adoption, leveraging policy support, local knowledge, and community partnerships.

5. Women as Innovators and Entrepreneurs

Women play a crucial role as innovators and entrepreneurs, driving economic growth, social change, and technological advancements. Despite facing systemic barriers, women-led businesses contribute significantly to job creation, sustainability, and inclusive leadership. Studies indicate that closing the gender gap in entrepreneurship could boost global GDP by 20%, highlighting the untapped potential of women entrepreneurs.

However, challenges such as limited access to funding, cultural biases, and restricted networks continue to hinder women's participation in innovation ecosystems. Initiatives like UN Women's WeEmpowerAsia program and gender-responsive investment funds aim to bridge these gaps by providing mentorship, financial support, and policy advocacy. Additionally, women-led startups are increasingly focusing on social impact, sustainability, and digital transformation, proving that innovation can drive both profitability and positive change.

Would you like insights on specific women-led innovation models or case studies? You can explore more details here, here, and here.

Across sectors and regions, women are driving innovation that reflects lived experiences and community needs. Examples include:

- **Health:** Female-led startups developing maternal health tracking apps and low-cost sanitary solutions.
- **Agriculture:** Women designing solar-powered irrigation systems and climate-smart farming tools tailored for small-scale women farmers.
- **Education:** Digital platforms that support girls' learning and mentorship in STEM fields.
- **Finance:** Women-led fintech initiatives that offer microloans and savings platforms to underserved women entrepreneurs.

These innovations are often social, inclusive, and impact-oriented—challenging conventional definitions of innovation that prioritize market disruption over social equity.

6. Case Studies in Inclusive Innovation

Scalability and sustainability are essential for advancing gender equality in innovation and entrepreneurship. Scalability ensures that gender-responsive initiatives can expand their impact, reaching more women and marginalized communities through strong institutional support, adaptable frameworks, and inclusive funding mechanisms. Sustainability, on the other hand, focuses on long-term viability, ensuring that gender-inclusive policies and programs remain effective beyond initial implementation. Organizations like ISEAL Alliance advocate for credible sustainability systems that integrate gender equality into business standards, environmental policies, and economic frameworks. Additionally, gender-transformative programs emphasize systemic change, ensuring that interventions are multiplicative, scalable, and sustainable. The UN Women

Pathways Approach highlights the need for intersectional strategies that align gender equality with sustainable development.

a. MIT D-Lab (Global)

MIT's D-Lab works with women in developing countries to co-create low-cost, high-impact technologies in energy, water, agriculture, and mobility.

b. Digital Green (India)

An agricultural platform that uses videos made by women farmers to share best practices, increasing adoption rates and local ownership.

c. Solar Sister (Africa)

A women-led enterprise that trains and supports women entrepreneurs to distribute solar lights and clean cookstoves in off-grid communities.

d. She Codes (Israel)

A network aimed at increasing the number of women in tech through free coding workshops and mentorship, fostering a pipeline of future innovators.

7. Policy and Institutional Support for Inclusive Innovation

Policy and institutional support play a crucial role in fostering inclusive innovation, ensuring that marginalized communities and underrepresented groups can actively participate in technological and economic advancements. Governments and organizations worldwide are implementing inclusive innovation policies that remove barriers for disadvantaged groups, promote equitable access to resources, and encourage diverse participation in research and entrepreneurship.

National innovation systems are being restructured to integrate gender-responsive frameworks, ensuring that women and minority entrepreneurs receive adequate funding, mentorship, and policy support. Additionally, institutions like UNESCO and OECD advocate for inclusive policy design, emphasizing the need for territorial, industrial, and social inclusiveness in innovation ecosystems.

Governments, academic institutions, and the private sector can support inclusive innovation through:

- **Gender-responsive innovation policies** that incentivize diversity in research teams and funding allocations.
- **Support for women-led startups,** including access to seed funding, accelerators, and venture capital.

- **STEM education and training** targeted at girls and women from early education through advanced research.
- **Innovation labs and tech hubs** that are safe, accessible, and inclusive spaces for women.
- **Data collection and metrics** that track gender-disaggregated innovation outcomes and inform policy.

8. Future Directions

The future of gender equality will be shaped by policy advancements, technological innovations, and evolving social norms. Emerging priorities include closing economic gaps, increasing women's representation in leadership, and addressing gender-based violence. The rise of digital activism and AI-driven solutions is transforming advocacy efforts, enabling more inclusive participation in decision-making. However, challenges such as the rollback of women's rights, climate change, and online harassment continue to pose significant obstacles.

Organizations and governments are focusing on gender-responsive budgeting, equitable access to education, and sustainable development strategies to drive long-term change. Additionally, intersectional approaches that consider race, disability, and socioeconomic status are becoming central to gender equality frameworks. The Equalities Resource Hub highlights key areas for future action, including strengthening legal protections, expanding economic opportunities, and fostering inclusive governance.

The future of innovation must be intentionally inclusive, intersectional, and co-designed. Key priorities include:

- **Mainstreaming inclusive innovation** into national development strategies.
- **Fostering public-private partnerships** that prioritize gender equity in technology and design.
- **Leveraging AI and emerging technologies** to close gender gaps rather than widen them.
- **Amplifying women's voices** in global innovation forums and leadership roles.

9. Conclusion

Inclusive innovation is not about creating "women's solutions"—it is about transforming innovation systems to be participatory, just, and representative of diverse human needs. Designing for and with women leads to better outcomes not only for women but for families, communities, and societies at large. Women's full participation in innovation is a cornerstone of inclusive growth and sustainable development.

References

- *UNESCO (2023). Cracking the Code: Girls' and Women's Education in STEM.*
- *World Bank (2022). Inclusive Innovation for Development.*
- *UN Women (2023). Gender and Innovation: A Policy Review.*
- *OECD (2021). Bridging the Gender Gap in Innovation and Entrepreneurship.*
- *D-Lab MIT. (2022). Inclusive Design for Development Toolkit.*

CHAPTER SIXTEEN

Youth and the Future of Feminist Leadership

Author: *Dr. Durgesh Singh, Assistant Consultant at Tata Consultancy Services, New Delhi, Delhi, India*

Abstract

This chapter explores the intersection of youth and feminist leadership, examining how the next generation of leaders is shaping the feminist movement. It highlights the unique perspectives and innovative approaches that young feminists bring to the table, emphasizing the importance of inclusivity, intersectionality, and digital activism. By analyzing current trends and future possibilities, this chapter aims to provide insights into how youth can lead the charge for a more equitable and just society.

Introduction

The landscape of feminist leadership is undergoing a profound transformation, driven in large part by the passion, creativity, and resilience of young people. No longer confined to the peripheries of activism, youth are emerging as central figures in the feminist movement—challenging traditional hierarchies, mobilizing communities, and championing more inclusive and intersectional approaches to justice. As the torchbearers of social change, young feminists are redefining what leadership looks like in the 21st century.

This chapter explores how youth are not only participating in feminist leadership but actively reshaping its direction. Through their lived experiences, values rooted in equity and inclusion, and strategic use of digital technologies, young leaders are forging new paths that prioritize collaboration, care, and systemic change. At the same time, they face unique challenges—from ageism and resource limitations to navigating online harassment—that must be acknowledged and addressed to ensure a truly inclusive and sustainable movement.

By centering the voices and visions of young feminists, this chapter highlights the urgent need to invest in, support, and learn from the next generation of leaders. Their leadership is not just the future of feminism—it is its present force and transformative engine.

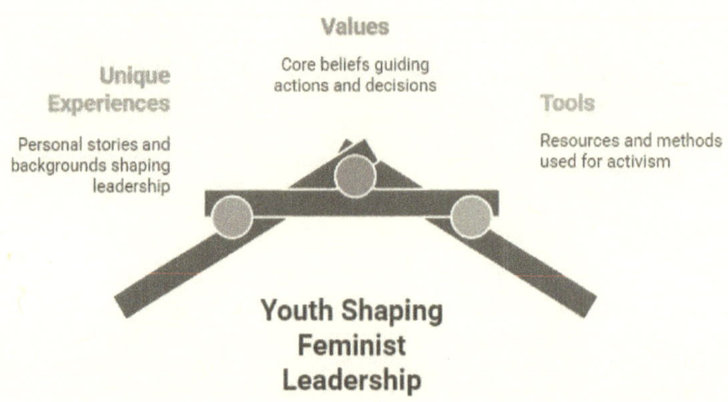

Youth Shaping Feminist Leadership

The Role of Youth in Feminist Movements
Historical Context

Historically, youth have played a pivotal role in social movements, often serving as catalysts for change. From the suffragette movement to the civil rights movement, young activists have consistently challenged the status quo. Today, this legacy continues as young feminists advocate for gender equality, reproductive rights, and social justice on a global scale.

Current Trends

In recent years, we have witnessed a surge in youth-led feminist initiatives. Movements such as #MeToo and #TimesUp have gained traction, largely due to the involvement of young activists who leverage social media platforms to amplify their voices. This digital activism allows for rapid mobilization and the dissemination of information, making it easier for youth to engage with and influence feminist discourse.

Key Characteristics of Youth Feminist Leadership
Inclusivity and Intersectionality

One of the defining features of youth-led feminist leadership is its commitment to inclusivity and intersectionality. Young feminists are increasingly aware of the diverse experiences and identities that shape women's lives. They advocate for a feminism that recognizes the interconnectedness of race, class, sexuality, and ability, ensuring that all voices are heard and represented.

Innovation and Creativity

Youth bring a fresh perspective to feminist leadership, often employing innovative strategies to address complex issues. Whether through art, technology, or grassroots organizing, young feminists are not afraid to think outside the box. This creativity is essential for engaging a broader audience and fostering a sense of community among activists.

Digital Activism

The rise of social media has transformed the way movements operate, and youth are adept at utilizing these platforms to promote their causes. Digital activism allows for real-time communication, collaboration, and mobilization, enabling young feminists to reach a global audience. This shift has also democratized leadership, allowing anyone with internet access to contribute to the feminist discourse.

Challenges Faced by Young Feminist Leaders

Young feminist leaders are at the forefront of transformative activism, bringing fresh perspectives, bold ideas, and a deep commitment to justice. However, they often face a unique set of challenges that can hinder their effectiveness and sustainability within the movement. Despite their strengths, young feminists encounter several challenges in their pursuit of leadership. These include:

Ageism

Despite their passion, creativity, and deep commitment to justice, young activists frequently encounter ageism within feminist spaces and broader social movements. Their ideas may be dismissed as naïve, their experiences undervalued, and their capabilities questioned by older generations who may view youth as lacking the necessary experience or strategic depth. This skepticism can create barriers to meaningful participation in decision-making processes and reinforce hierarchical power dynamics that exclude emerging leaders from shaping agendas and policies.

Ageism not only stifles innovation but also undermines the feminist principle of inclusivity. It can discourage intergenerational mentorship, reduce confidence among young leaders, and perpetuate cycles of disempowerment. To counter this, feminist spaces must cultivate a culture of mutual respect, where knowledge flows in both directions—recognizing the value of lived experiences across age groups. By dismantling ageist attitudes and embracing youth leadership as vital to the movement's evolution, we can build a more equitable and resilient feminist future.

Resource Limitations

Many youth-led feminist initiatives are driven by passion, innovation, and a deep commitment to social justice—but often operate with minimal financial support. Limited budgets, inadequate access to institutional funding, and heavy reliance on volunteer labor can significantly constrain their capacity to implement large-scale programs or sustain long-term impact. This lack of resources not only affects operational stability but also limits opportunities for leadership development, outreach, and organizational growth.

Additionally, bureaucratic barriers and funding models that favor established organizations can further marginalize youth-led efforts, especially those led by young women, queer individuals, and activists from the Global South. Addressing these resource limitations requires intentional investment in youth leadership, flexible funding mechanisms, and partnerships that prioritize equity and trust. By ensuring that young feminists have the tools, funding, and institutional support they need, we can unlock their full potential and amplify their contributions to transformative social change.

Navigating Online Spaces

Digital platforms have become powerful tools for feminist activism, enabling rapid mobilization, global solidarity, and the amplification of marginalized voices. However, these online spaces also present significant challenges. Young feminists often face targeted harassment, cyberbullying, and threats that seek to silence their advocacy and undermine their confidence. The spread of misinformation and disinformation can distort feminist messages and derail important conversations, while algorithmic biases may limit the visibility of critical content.

In addition, the pressure to maintain a constant online presence—curating content, responding to engagement, and staying up-to-date—can be emotionally and mentally taxing, often leading to burnout. Navigating these spaces requires digital literacy, robust support systems, and strategies for self-care and collective care. To sustain their activism, young feminists need access to digital safety training, mental health resources, and networks of solidarity that prioritize well-being alongside impact. By addressing these challenges head-on, the feminist movement can continue to thrive in the digital age without compromising the health and security of its leaders.

The Future of Feminist Leadership

The future of feminist leadership lies in its ability to be inclusive, adaptive, and visionary. As the world faces complex challenges—from climate change and digital surveillance to deepening social inequalities—feminist leadership must evolve to address these intersecting issues through a justice-oriented lens. Central to this future is the cultivation of diverse leadership that reflects a broad spectrum of identities, experiences, and geographies.

Young leaders, especially those from marginalized communities, must be empowered with resources, mentorship, and platforms that enable them to lead authentically and effectively. Intergenerational collaboration will also be key, ensuring that the wisdom of past struggles informs present actions while embracing fresh perspectives and approaches.

Moreover, feminist leadership must remain dynamic, open to change, and grounded in solidarity. It should embrace innovation, harness technology for social good, and challenge traditional power structures not only in society but within the movement itself. By doing so, feminist leadership can remain a transformative force, capable of inspiring collective action and creating a more equitable and just world for all.

Youth Leadership in Feminism

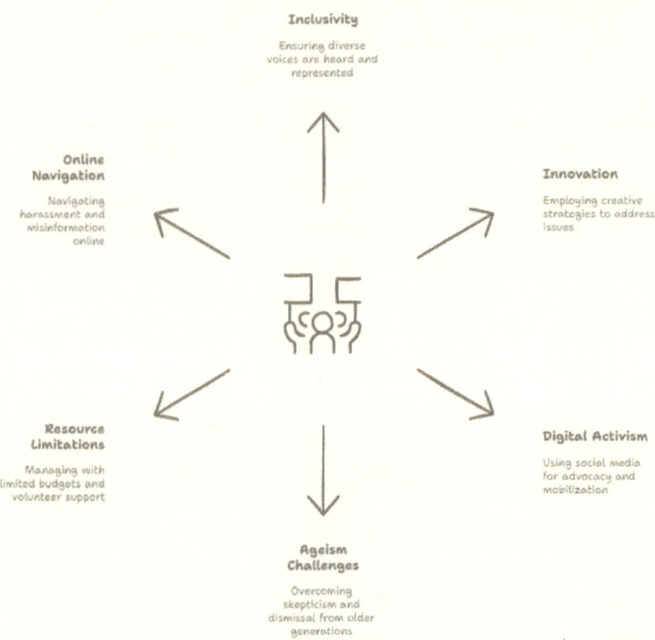

Youth Leadership in Feminism

Empowering Young Leaders

To secure a vibrant and sustainable future for feminist leadership, it is essential to invest in and empower young leaders. This involves creating structured mentorship programs that connect emerging voices with experienced feminists who can provide guidance, support, and institutional knowledge. Additionally, providing equitable access to funding, scholarships, and leadership training enables young women and gender-diverse individuals to pursue initiatives that drive change in their communities. Platforms—both digital and physical—that amplify their voices are equally important, offering spaces for expression, collaboration, and visibility. By nurturing young leaders through these avenues, we not only build capacity for the future but also enrich the feminist movement with fresh perspectives, energy, and innovation.

Fostering Collaboration

Intergenerational collaboration is vital for the continued growth and resilience of the feminist movement. By fostering mutual respect and open dialogue between seasoned feminists and emerging leaders, the movement can bridge historical knowledge with contemporary insights. Experienced activists bring a wealth of lived experience, strategic know-how, and lessons learned from past struggles, while younger feminists contribute innovative ideas, digital fluency, and fresh approaches to advocacy. This exchange not only strengthens the collective impact of the movement but also promotes inclusivity, ensuring that diverse voices across age groups are heard, valued, and empowered. Through intentional collaboration, the feminist movement can remain adaptive, united, and forward-looking.

Embracing Change

The future of feminist leadership depends on its capacity to evolve alongside shifting societal, political, and technological landscapes. As new challenges and opportunities emerge—ranging from digital activism to intersectional justice—feminist strategies must remain flexible, innovative, and inclusive. Embracing change means being open to reimagining traditional approaches, integrating diverse voices, and leveraging new tools for advocacy and outreach. It also requires a willingness to question internal practices and adapt to the needs of marginalized communities within the movement. By staying responsive and forward-thinking, feminist leadership can sustain its momentum, remain relevant, and drive transformative, long-term impact.

Conclusion

Youth are not just the leaders of tomorrow; they are the leaders of today. As they continue to shape the future of feminist leadership, it is imperative that we listen to their voices, support their initiatives, and recognize the invaluable contributions they make to the movement. By fostering an environment that encourages innovation, inclusivity, and collaboration, we can ensure that feminist leadership remains relevant and effective in the pursuit of gender equality and social justice.

Reference:

- *Kenny, L., McIlwaine, C., & Talcott, M. (2020). Feminist activism and young people: Emerging pathways in the global South and North. Routledge.*

CHAPTER SEVENTEEN

Leadership and Representation of Women in Tech Industries

Author: Swati Singh, *Assistant Professor at Vardhaman College of Engineering, Hyderabad, Telangana*

Abstract

The technology sector, a driving force of global innovation and economic growth, has long suffered from gender disparity in leadership and representation. This chapter explores the current landscape of women's participation in tech, highlighting structural barriers, cultural biases, and institutional gaps that hinder their advancement. Drawing from global data, case studies, and research, it examines strategies for cultivating inclusive tech environments and strengthening leadership pipelines for women. It argues that achieving gender parity in technology leadership is not only a moral imperative but also essential for fostering diversity-driven innovation and sustainable industry growth.

Keywords: gender diversity, women in tech, leadership, representation, STEM, inclusion, technology sector, digital economy

1. Introduction

The digital revolution has reshaped economies, societies, and the future of work—yet women remain underrepresented, especially in leadership roles across technology industries. While efforts to improve gender diversity in STEM fields have gained momentum, the upper echelons of tech companies continue to be dominated by men. Representation matters: women leaders in tech serve as role models, drive inclusive product design, and shape equitable workplace cultures. This chapter examines the state of women's leadership in tech, identifies barriers to advancement, and proposes strategies to close the gender gap.

2. Current Landscape

The technology sector, often heralded as the engine of innovation and economic growth, presents a paradox when it comes to gender inclusion. Despite the growing emphasis on diversity and equity, women remain significantly underrepresented, particularly in technical and leadership roles. This section outlines the current status of women in the tech industry, focusing on workforce participation, representation in leadership, and intersectional disparities.

2.1 Participation Rates

Globally, women make up between 28% and 35% of the total workforce in the technology sector, with the proportion varying by region and sub-sector. In developed economies like the United States, women occupy roughly 25% of computing jobs, and this number has remained relatively stagnant over the past decade (NCWIT, 2023). In many developing countries, participation rates are even lower due to limited access to education and systemic socio-economic barriers.

Within the tech workforce, women are often concentrated in non-technical or support roles such as human resources, marketing, and project coordination, rather than core areas like software development, data science, or systems engineering.

2.2 Leadership Disparities

When it comes to leadership, the representation of women diminishes sharply. According to the AnitaB.org 2023 report, women held only 18% of senior leadership roles in tech companies, and less than 10% of Chief Technology Officer (CTO) positions. Fortune 500 companies reflect a similar trend—only a small fraction of tech firms are led by women CEOs or have gender-balanced executive boards.

In venture capital and startup ecosystems, the disparity is more pronounced: less than 3% of venture capital funding goes to all-women founding teams, and women-led startups often receive smaller investments even when their performance metrics are equal or better than male-led counterparts.

2.3 Intersectionality and Inclusion Gaps

The challenges faced by women in tech are exacerbated by intersectionality—where factors such as race, ethnicity, disability, and socioeconomic background intersect with gender. For example, Black and

Latina women hold less than 5% of computing roles in the United States and are even less represented in leadership. Similarly, women with disabilities, LGBTQ+ individuals, and those from rural or marginalized communities often experience heightened exclusion.

2.4 Organizational Culture and Retention

Retention is another pressing issue. Women in tech leave the industry at twice the rate of men, often due to hostile work environments, lack of advancement opportunities, and work-life balance challenges. The so-called "leaky pipeline" means that even when women enter the tech sector, systemic barriers push them out before they can reach senior roles.

According to a 2022 report by Accenture and Girls Who Code, improving workplace culture could boost the number of women in tech roles by 3 million in the U.S. alone.

3. Barriers to Leadership

Despite progress in awareness and advocacy, systemic barriers continue to hinder women's advancement into leadership roles in the tech industry. These barriers are rooted in cultural biases, institutional practices, and structural inequalities that cumulatively disadvantage women over the course of their careers. This section outlines the key obstacles that contribute to the leadership gap.

- **3.1 Gender Bias and Stereotypes** Persistent gender stereotypes suggest that men are more naturally suited to technical roles and leadership positions. These biases shape recruitment, promotion, and performance evaluation practices. Women in tech often face the "prove-it-again" phenomenon, where they must constantly demonstrate their competence in ways that their male counterparts are not required to do. Moreover, the "double bind" places women in a no-win situation: assertiveness is seen as abrasive, while collaboration may be perceived as weakness. These stereotypes affect how women are perceived as leaders and can limit their upward mobility.

- **3.2 Work-Life Integration Challenges** Mentorship and sponsorship are essential for career advancement, yet women—particularly those from marginalized backgrounds—often lack access to influential mentors or sponsors who can advocate for them in high-stakes decision-making environments. While mentorship offers guidance and support, sponsorship involves active promotion and opportunity creation, which is critical for ascending to leadership roles. The scarcity of women in senior positions also creates a "representation bottleneck," reducing opportunities for younger women to find role models who reflect their experiences.

- **3.3 Lack of Mentorship and Sponsorship** In tech industries, career advancement often depends not only on merit but also on access to informal networks—social circles where important decisions are made and opportunities are shared. Women are frequently excluded from these networks due to gendered social dynamics, making it harder to gain visibility or access strategic projects. This exclusion can be even more pronounced for women of color, LGBTQ+ individuals, or those from underrepresented socioeconomic backgrounds, who may experience a double or triple exclusion.

- **3.4 Work-Life Integration Challenges** The tech sector often rewards long hours, constant availability, and "always-on" work cultures. These expectations disproportionately affect women, particularly those with caregiving responsibilities. Inadequate family leave policies, lack of affordable childcare, and rigid work schedules create a significant barrier to leadership for women balancing professional and personal obligations. Although remote work and flexible schedules have become more common, they do not automatically translate into equitable career advancement if women are still perceived as less committed or visible.

- **3.5 Organizational Culture and Microaggressions** Toxic or exclusionary work environments also hinder women's progress. Reports of gender-based microaggressions, unequal pay, limited opportunities for advancement, and even sexual harassment continue to surface in tech companies across the globe. A culture that tolerates or ignores such issues erodes confidence, reduces retention, and creates psychological barriers for women aspiring to leadership roles.

- **3.6 Structural and Policy Gaps** Many organizations lack transparent and gender-sensitive promotion practices. Without clear criteria or accountability systems, unconscious bias can influence who is considered "leadership material." Furthermore, the absence of diversity goals, inclusive hiring practices, and gender-disaggregated data makes it difficult to track progress and identify gaps.

4. Advancing Women's Leadership in Tech

Addressing the leadership gap in technology requires a comprehensive and systemic approach. Efforts must go beyond recruitment to include retention, promotion, and the transformation of workplace culture. This section explores key strategies and initiatives to advance women's leadership in the tech industry.

4.1 Building Inclusive Pipelines

Building inclusive pipelines for women in tech starts with early exposure to STEM education through school programs, coding bootcamps, and hands-on learning opportunities that challenge gender stereotypes and spark interest in technology. Targeted scholarships and financial aid for women—especially those from underrepresented and marginalized communities—help reduce barriers to higher education and signal institutional commitment to equity. Alternative pathways such as coding bootcamps and online certifications offer accessible routes into tech careers, particularly for those without traditional degrees. Focused outreach to women of color, LGBTQ+ individuals, and those in rural or low-income areas ensures a more diverse pipeline. Additionally, increasing the visibility of female role models in tech and offering mentorship opportunities can inspire young women and affirm that leadership in technology is both attainable and valued. These integrated efforts, spanning education, industry, and policy, are essential to cultivating a diverse and resilient tech workforce.

4.2 Corporate Commitments and Accountability

For meaningful progress in advancing women's leadership in tech, companies must shift from symbolic gestures to concrete, measurable actions that foster equity and inclusion. This begins with embedding gender equity into the organizational core through transparent hiring and promotion criteria that reduce bias and establish clear pathways to advancement. Regular gender-equity audits—assessing pay equity, representation at all levels, and employee experiences—are essential for identifying gaps and guiding corrective action. Setting and publicly reporting on measurable diversity targets for recruitment, retention, and leadership roles helps ensure accountability and drives cultural change. Moreover, performance evaluations for senior leaders should include diversity outcomes as key metrics. When corporate strategies are aligned with accountability mechanisms, they move from intention to impact, creating workplaces where women not only enter but also thrive and lead.

4.3 Supporting Women Entrepreneurs in Tech

Supporting women entrepreneurs in technology is critical to fostering innovation, inclusion, and economic growth. Despite their potential, women-led startups receive a disproportionately small share of venture capital funding, often due to systemic bias, limited networks, and a lack of visibility. Addressing this gap requires targeted investment through gender-responsive venture capital, dedicated accelerators, and inclusive incubator programs that provide access to capital, resources, and strategic mentorship. Initiatives such as All Raise, Women Who Tech, and Female Founders Fund are leading the way by building ecosystems that connect women founders with investors, advisors, and peers. Additionally, public-private partnerships and government-backed innovation funds can further amplify support by prioritizing diversity in tech entrepreneurship. Empowering women in the startup space not only unlocks underutilized talent but also leads to more inclusive products and services that better reflect the needs of diverse users.

4.4 Leadership Development and Networking

Leadership development and strong professional networks are essential for advancing women in the tech industry. Structured programs—such as leadership academies, executive training, and career acceleration initiatives—equip women with critical skills in strategic thinking, negotiation, and decision-making. These programs often address the unique challenges women face in male-dominated environments, offering tailored support to build confidence and executive presence. Organizations like AnitaB.org, Women in Technology International (WITI), and Lean In Circles provide platforms for mentorship, peer learning, and visibility, fostering a sense of community and shared growth. Networking opportunities through conferences, workshops, and industry alliances not only expand professional connections but also open doors to leadership roles, board positions, and venture funding. By investing in leadership development and inclusive networking, the tech industry can cultivate a diverse pipeline of women leaders equipped to shape the future of innovation.

5. Case Studies

India's Women Techmakers Program (Google): The Women Techmakers program by Google in India serves as a vital platform to empower women in technology by offering visibility, community support, and essential resources. Launched to address gender imbalances in the tech industry, the initiative provides women with access to speaking opportunities, technical training, and leadership workshops that help elevate their professional profiles. Through events like International

Women's Day celebrations, hackathons, and summits, Women Techmakers fosters a vibrant community where women can share knowledge, collaborate on projects, and build lasting networks. The program also offers online resources, mentorship, and scholarship opportunities, making it a comprehensive support system for aspiring and established women tech professionals. By promoting inclusivity and amplifying the voices of women in tech across India, Women Techmakers is contributing to a more diverse and dynamic technology ecosystem.

Black Girls CODE (USA): Black Girls CODE is a pioneering nonprofit organization dedicated to empowering girls of color to become leaders and innovators in STEM fields through coding education and mentorship. By providing hands-on workshops, after-school programs, and hackathons, Black Girls CODE creates accessible pathways for young women—especially African American and other underrepresented minorities—to develop critical technical skills in computer programming, robotics, and game development. Beyond skill-building, the organization fosters a supportive community that boosts confidence, encourages creativity, and cultivates leadership. Mentorship from women professionals in tech offers role models who inspire and guide participants toward careers in technology and engineering. Since its inception, Black Girls CODE has reached thousands of girls across the United States, helping to close the diversity gap in STEM and transform the future of tech innovation through inclusion and empowerment.

She Loves Tech (Global):
She Loves Tech is the world's largest startup competition and accelerator platform dedicated to women-led and women-impact tech startups. Operating in over 80 countries and having supported more than 15,000 startups, the initiative aims to close the gender funding gap and empower women entrepreneurs globally .Startup Daily+1Women in Tech Network.

The program offers a comprehensive ecosystem that includes global pitch competitions, mentorship, investor matching, and capacity-building workshops. Finalists participate in a week-long bootcamp and showcase their ventures at the Global Final Summit in Singapore, connecting with investors and industry leaders .shelovestech.org.

In addition to the competition, She Loves Tech operates the She Loves Tech Fund and She Loves Tech Alliance, which bring together world-class investors to catalyze investments in women-led startups .shelovestech.org.

Through its initiatives, She Loves Tech has facilitated over $500 million in funding for women-led ventures, impacting sectors such as health tech, fintech, edtech, and climate tech .shelovestech.org

By providing visibility, resources, and a global network, She Loves Tech plays a pivotal role in transforming the landscape for women entrepreneurs in technology.

6. Conclusion

Elevating women in tech leadership is not just about achieving gender parity—it is about unlocking innovation, creativity, and economic potential. As the technology sector shapes the future of society, it must reflect the diversity of the people it serves. Addressing systemic barriers, investing in inclusive leadership pipelines, and fostering equitable workplace cultures are key steps toward a truly inclusive digital economy.

References

1. *NCWIT. (2023). Women in Tech: The Facts. National Center for Women & Information Technology.*
2. *McKinsey & Company. (2020). Diversity Wins: How Inclusion Matters.*
3. *UNESCO. (2021). Cracking the Code: Girls' and Women's Education in STEM.*
4. *World Economic Forum. (2022). Global Gender Gap Report.*
5. *AnitaB.org. (2023). Top Companies for Women Technologists.*

CHAPTER EIGHTEEN

Women Leading Economic Change

Author: *Sarvesh Singh, Assistant Professor at Department of Management, Oriental College of Technology, Bhopal, Madhya Pradesh*

Abstract

This chapter explores the pivotal role of women in driving economic change across diverse sectors and regions. It highlights how women's leadership—through entrepreneurship, corporate governance, policymaking, and grassroots activism—contributes to more inclusive and sustainable economic development. Drawing on global case studies and current data, the chapter examines both the progress made and the systemic barriers that persist, such as gender biases, unequal access to resources, and policy gaps. It also outlines strategic interventions that can empower women and amplify their impact. The discussion underscores that empowering women economically is not only a matter of equity but also a critical lever for social transformation and economic resilience.

Keywords

Women's economic empowerment, gender equality, inclusive growth, female leadership, entrepreneurship, microfinance, digital inclusion, economic development, policy reform, structural inequality.

Introduction

In the twenty-first century, women have emerged not just as participants but as pivotal leaders in economic transformation globally. From entrepreneurship and corporate leadership to policymaking and grassroots activism, women's roles in reshaping economies are increasingly recognized as fundamental to inclusive and sustainable growth. This chapter explores the multifaceted contributions of women to economic change, analyzes the systemic barriers they continue to face, and highlights transformative strategies that amplify their impact.

The Global Context of Women in Economic Leadership

Despite significant advancements in gender equality, disparities persist in economic leadership roles. According to the World Economic Forum's Global Gender Gap Report, women globally hold only about 30% of senior managerial positions. However, countries and organizations that have prioritized gender diversity in leadership report higher innovation, better decision-making, and improved financial performance.

Economic change driven by women is not limited to the corporate boardroom. Women are leaders in microfinance initiatives, cooperative enterprises, and digital marketplaces, particularly in the Global South. Their contributions often extend beyond economic metrics to include social cohesion, environmental sustainability, and community resilience.

Key Drivers of Women's Economic Leadership

The growing influence of women in economic spheres is propelled by a confluence of structural shifts, technological advances, and socio-political movements. Understanding the key drivers of women's economic leadership is essential to both appreciating their contributions and identifying areas for targeted intervention and support. These drivers are diverse and interconnected, ranging from entrepreneurship and corporate governance to digital inclusion and community engagement.

1. Entrepreneurship and Innovation

Women entrepreneurs are spearheading new business models that challenge traditional industry norms and create inclusive economic opportunities. In regions like Sub-Saharan Africa and South Asia, women-led enterprises constitute a significant portion of the informal economy, driving both employment and innovation.

Digital platforms have democratized access to markets, allowing women to bypass traditional gatekeepers. For instance, e-commerce has enabled women in rural areas to sell products globally, increasing income and independence.

- **Impact:** Women-led businesses are more likely to reinvest profits in their communities, health, and education, contributing to broader socio-economic development.
- **Enablers:** Access to microfinance, digital tools, and incubator programs has played a critical role in fostering women's entrepreneurship, especially in developing economies.

2. Corporate and Institutional Leadership

Women at the helm of corporations and institutions bring unique leadership styles that emphasize collaboration, empathy, and ethical governance. Studies suggest that companies with gender-diverse leadership outperform their peers in profitability and sustainability metrics.

Progress in gender parity in corporate leadership has been driven by policies such as gender quotas, mentorship programs, and family-friendly workplace practices. However, persistent glass ceilings and gender biases continue to hinder equal representation.

- **Impact:** Research shows a positive correlation between gender-diverse leadership teams and higher financial performance, improved ESG outcomes, and stronger crisis management.
- **Enablers:** Board quotas, mentorship initiatives, and leadership development programs have been effective in promoting gender balance at the top.

3. Policy Influence and Advocacy

Women in political and policy-making roles have championed reforms that promote economic equity, such as parental leave, childcare support, and pay equity laws. Their leadership often intersects with broader social justice movements, amplifying the voice of marginalized groups.

Grassroots women's organizations have also been instrumental in mobilizing communities for economic justice, advocating for land rights, fair wages, and access to credit.

Case Studies

A. Grameen Bank and Microfinance in Bangladesh

Founded by Nobel Laureate Muhammad Yunus, the Grameen Bank's model of microcredit was revolutionary, particularly in empowering rural women. Women borrowers not only repaid loans at higher rates but also invested in their families' education, health, and well-being, triggering intergenerational economic benefits.

B. Female Leadership in Nordic Countries

Nordic countries consistently rank high in gender equality indices, owing partly to strong female representation in government and business. Policies supporting parental leave, universal childcare, and workplace equality have created environments where women can thrive economically.

C. Digital Inclusion in Kenya

M-Pesa, a mobile phone-based money transfer service, has significantly impacted women's economic participation in Kenya. Women entrepreneurs use mobile banking to manage finances, access credit, and build savings—tools that are critical for scaling their businesses.

Barriers to Economic Participation

Despite notable progress in promoting women's economic empowerment globally, systemic and multifaceted barriers continue to limit their full and equitable participation in the economy. These barriers are deeply rooted in historical inequalities, institutional structures, and socio-cultural norms, and they vary across regions, income levels, and industries. Addressing them is essential not only for gender justice but for realizing inclusive and sustainable economic growth.

Despite progress, women face persistent challenges:

Despite significant strides in education, legal reform, and representation, women continue to face deeply entrenched challenges that inhibit their full participation in economic life.

Structural Inequality: Limited access to education, finance, and property significantly restricts women's economic agency and autonomy. In many regions, girls receive fewer years of schooling than boys, particularly in rural or marginalized communities, limiting their opportunities for skilled employment. Financial exclusion remains pervasive—women are less likely to have bank accounts, access credit, or receive investment capital, often due to lack of collateral or discriminatory lending practices. Furthermore, legal and cultural barriers often prevent women from owning or inheriting land and property, which are essential assets for wealth creation and business development. These structural inequalities compound over time, perpetuating cycles of poverty and dependence.

Cultural Norms and Gender Roles: Deeply ingrained societal expectations often confine women to traditional roles as caregivers and homemakers, assigning them a disproportionate share of unpaid care and domestic work. This "time poverty" limits their ability to pursue education, employment, or entrepreneurship. In many cultures, women who seek economic independence or leadership positions face social stigma, familial resistance, or community backlash, which can undermine confidence and ambition. These gendered expectations not only restrict individual potential but also hinder broader economic development by underutilizing half of the population's talent and capacity.

Violence and Discrimination: Gender-based violence—both in private and public spheres—remains a significant barrier to women's economic participation. Workplace harassment, including sexual intimidation and coercion, creates hostile environments that drive women out of the workforce or prevent them from advancing. Domestic violence further restricts mobility, access to employment, and financial independence. In addition, discriminatory practices such as biased hiring, unequal pay, and lack of legal protections erode women's confidence, safety, and long-term economic security. These forms of violence and discrimination are not only human rights violations but also economic constraints that limit productivity and growth at societal levels.

Policy Gaps: In many countries, inadequate or outdated legal frameworks fail to safeguard women's economic rights and promote equal opportunities. Critical areas such as equal pay, maternity leave, workplace harassment, and inheritance rights often lack comprehensive legislation or effective enforcement. Even where progressive laws exist, implementation is frequently weak due to limited political will, lack of awareness, or insufficient institutional capacity. Moreover, economic policies and budgets are rarely gender-responsive, overlooking the distinct needs and contributions of women. These gaps leave women vulnerable to exploitation, limit their participation in formal economies, and perpetuate systemic inequality. Addressing policy gaps is essential to creating inclusive and equitable economic systems.

Strategies for Empowerment and Change

Empowering women economically requires deliberate, multi-dimensional strategies that dismantle barriers, promote equity, and foster leadership. These strategies must be grounded in inclusivity, sustainability, and systemic reform, with the active participation of governments, private sector actors, civil society, and women themselves. Below are key approaches that have proven effective in advancing women's economic empowerment and leadership.

To sustain and scale women's economic leadership, targeted interventions are needed:

To sustain and scale women's economic leadership, targeted interventions are needed that address both immediate barriers and long-term structural challenges. These interventions must be comprehensive, context-specific, and inclusive of women's voices at every stage.

Invest in Girls' Education: Empowerment begins with education, which equips girls and young women with the knowledge, skills, and confidence necessary to participate fully in economic life. Prioritizing education—especially in science, technology, engineering, and mathematics (STEM) as well as business and entrepreneurship—prepares girls for high-demand, well-paying careers and leadership roles. Education also fosters critical thinking, problem-solving, and digital literacy, essential skills in today's rapidly evolving economies. Moreover, educated girls are more likely to delay marriage and childbearing, improve health outcomes for themselves and their families, and become agents of change in their communities. Investing in girls' education is, therefore, a foundational strategy for sustainable economic empowerment and gender equality.

Expand Access to Finance: Inclusive banking and gender-sensitive credit programs are critical to unlocking women's economic potential. Despite their entrepreneurial spirit and contributions, women frequently encounter barriers to accessing formal financial services, including lack of collateral, limited credit histories, and discriminatory lending practices. Expanding access means designing financial products and services that meet women's unique needs—such as microloans, flexible repayment schedules, and group lending models—that can help overcome these obstacles. Fintech innovations like mobile banking and digital wallets have also proven transformative by reaching women in remote or underserved areas, allowing them to save securely, receive payments, and build credit histories. Additionally, financial literacy programs tailored to women increase their confidence and ability to manage money, invest in businesses, and plan for the future. By fostering an inclusive financial ecosystem, economies can empower women entrepreneurs, improve household welfare, and stimulate broader economic growth.

Support Women-Led Enterprises: Governments and the private sector play a vital role in nurturing women-led enterprises by prioritizing procurement, investment, and capacity-building tailored to their unique challenges. Women entrepreneurs often face difficulties accessing markets, financing, and networks that are essential for growth and scalability. Public procurement policies that set targets or quotas for sourcing from women-owned businesses can open substantial market opportunities and incentivize private sector engagement. Similarly, investment funds and venture capital initiatives that specifically target women-led startups help bridge the gender financing gap, fueling innovation and job creation.

Beyond capital, technical assistance, mentorship programs, and business development services provide critical support to build entrepreneurial skills, improve management capacity, and expand market reach. By fostering an enabling ecosystem, stakeholders can empower women entrepreneurs to become dynamic drivers of economic growth and inclusive development.

Foster Inclusive Workplaces: Creating inclusive workplaces is essential to ensuring that women can thrive professionally and contribute fully to economic growth. Key measures include enforcing equal pay for equal work, which addresses persistent wage gaps and recognizes women's contributions fairly. Implementing comprehensive parental leave policies—for both mothers and fathers—supports work-life balance, reduces career interruptions, and promotes shared caregiving responsibilities. Additionally, robust anti-discrimination and anti-harassment policies are critical to fostering safe, respectful work environments that empower women and prevent gender-based violence and bias. Inclusive workplaces also benefit from flexible work arrangements, professional development opportunities, and transparent promotion pathways that mitigate systemic barriers women face. When organizations prioritize equity and dignity, they not only enhance employee satisfaction and retention but also improve innovation, productivity, and overall business performance.

Promote Leadership Pipelines: Building strong leadership pipelines is crucial to increasing women's representation in decision-making positions across sectors. Structured mentorship programs connect emerging women leaders with experienced role models who provide guidance, encouragement, and access to influential networks. Leadership training tailored to women's unique challenges enhances skills in strategic thinking, negotiation, and confidence-building, preparing them to navigate complex organizational dynamics. Additionally, fostering professional networks and peer support groups creates platforms for knowledge exchange, collaboration, and advocacy. Organizations and governments can further accelerate progress by implementing succession planning that identifies and nurtures high-potential women talent, and by setting transparent targets for gender diversity in leadership roles. By investing in these pipelines, societies unlock the full potential of women leaders who drive innovation, inclusivity, and sustainable economic change.

Conclusion

Women are not just beneficiaries of economic development—they are architects of it. As leaders, innovators, and changemakers, women are redefining the global economic landscape. Realizing the full potential of women's economic leadership requires dismantling structural barriers and cultivating ecosystems that support and sustain their agency. Inclusive economies are stronger economies, and the future of global prosperity depends on harnessing the power of women leading economic change.

References

1. Acker, J. (2006). Inequality Regimes: Gender, Class, and Race in Organizations. Gender & Society, 20(4), 441–464. https://doi.org/10.1177/0891243206289499

2. Asian Development Bank. (2021). Gender Equality and Women's Empowerment. https://www.adb.org/themes/gender/main

3. Blackden, M., & Wodon, Q. (2006). Gender, Time Use, and Poverty in Sub-Saharan Africa. World Bank Policy Research Working Paper, No. 73. https://documents.worldbank.org/curated/en/460091468308763166/Gender-time-use-and-poverty-in-Sub-Saharan-Africa

4. CARE International. (2019). The Business Case for Women's Economic Empowerment. https://www.care.org/our-impact/womens-economic-empowerment

5. International Labour Organization. (2018). Women at Work: Trends 2016-2017. https://www.ilo.org/global/publications/books/WCMS_457317/lang--en/index.htm

6. Kabeer, N. (2016). Gender Equality, Economic Growth, and Women's Agency: The "Endless Variety" and "Monotonous Similarity" of Patriarchal Constraints. Feminist Economics, 22(1), 295–321. https://doi.org/10.1080/13545701.2015.1090009

7. McKinsey Global Institute. (2020). The Power of Parity: Advancing Women's Equality in the United States. https://www.mckinsey.com/featured-insights/diversity-and-inclusion/the-power-of-parity-advancing-womens-equality-in-the-united-states

8. OECD. (2017). The Pursuit of Gender Equality: An Uphill Battle. OECD Publishing. https://doi.org/10.1787/9789264281318-en

9. World Bank. (2019). Women, Business and the Law 2019: A Decade of Reform. Washington, DC: World Bank. https://openknowledge.worldbank.org/handle/10986/31327

10. *World Economic Forum. (2022). Global Gender Gap Report 2022. https://www.weforum.org/reports/global-gender-gap-report-2022*

11. *UN Women. (2020). Progress of the World's Women 2019-2020: Families in a Changing World. https://www.unwomen.org/en/digital-library/publications/2019/06/progress-of-the-worlds-women-2019-2020*

CHAPTER NINETEEN

Breaking Barriers: Women in Growth

Author: Dr.Shagun Chahal, Assistant Professor at the School of Management & Commerce, Manav Rachna University, Faridabad

Abstract

Women's participation in economic growth is vital to achieving inclusive development, yet persistent barriers often limit their contribution. This chapter explores the multifaceted obstacles women face in accessing growth opportunities and presents strategies for breaking these barriers. It highlights how empowering women through education, entrepreneurship, financial inclusion, and leadership development can accelerate economic progress. The chapter also discusses policy reforms, cultural shifts, and innovations that foster environments where women can thrive as agents of growth. By showcasing global examples and evidence-based interventions, this chapter underscores the critical role of women in driving sustainable and equitable economic expansion.

Keywords

Women's economic growth, gender barriers, entrepreneurship, financial inclusion, leadership, gender equality, economic empowerment, policy reforms, sustainable development.

1. Introduction

Economic growth that excludes women is incomplete and less sustainable. Women constitute half of the world's population, yet their participation in growth sectors remains uneven and underleveraged. The challenge is to identify and dismantle the barriers hindering women's full involvement in economic expansion and to promote mechanisms that enable their growth as entrepreneurs, leaders, and skilled professionals.

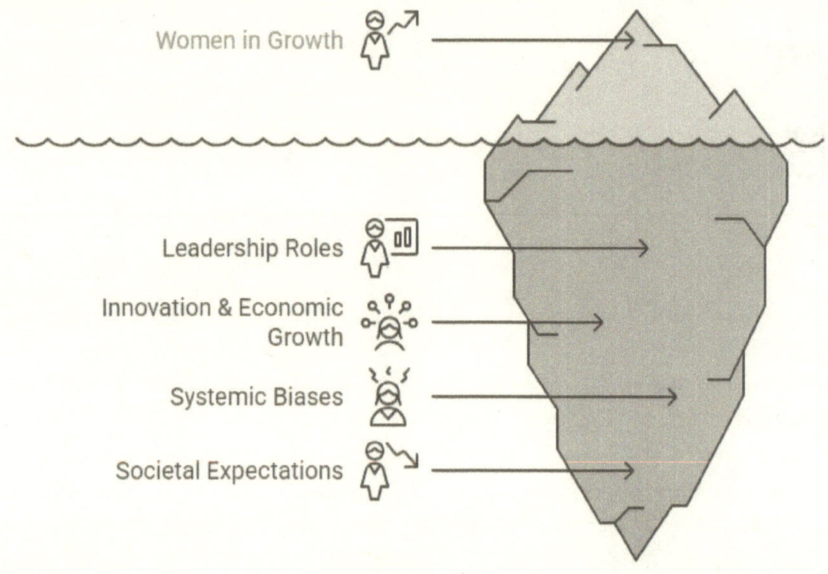

Breaking Barriers: Women in Growth

2. The Landscape of Women and Economic Growth

2.1 Women's Contribution to Growth

Women play a fundamental role in driving economic growth worldwide. Their participation in the labor force, entrepreneurial ventures, and leadership positions contributes significantly to innovation, productivity, and poverty alleviation. According to the McKinsey Global Institute (2015), closing the gender gap in labor force participation could add up to $28 trillion to global GDP by 2025. Women's economic activities span formal and informal sectors, from agriculture and manufacturing to technology and services, making them indispensable contributors to diverse economies. Moreover, women often reinvest earnings into their families and communities, amplifying the developmental impact of their economic engagement.

2.2 Persistent Barriers

Despite progress, women continue to face structural, cultural, and institutional barriers—including limited access to education, finance, markets, and decision-making power—that stymie their ability to contribute fully to economic growth. These barriers operate at multiple levels:

- **Structural Barriers:** Women often have less access to education, skill development, finance, and productive resources such as land and technology. Legal restrictions and discriminatory practices further restrict their rights to own property, enter contracts, or start businesses.
- **Cultural and Social Norms:** Gender stereotypes and traditional roles assign women primary responsibility for unpaid care work, limiting time and opportunities for economic participation. Societal expectations frequently discourage women from pursuing careers or leadership roles in certain industries.
- **Institutional Barriers:** Workplace discrimination, lack of family-friendly policies, and gender biases in hiring and promotion impede women's career progression and leadership representation.
- **Financial Exclusion:** Women face significant hurdles in accessing credit and financial services due to lack of collateral, gender-biased lending practices, and limited financial literacy.
- **Limited Networks and Mentorship:** Women entrepreneurs and professionals often lack access to influential networks, mentors, and role models that are crucial for business growth and career advancement.

These barriers create a complex web of constraints that contribute to the persistent gender gaps in economic participation, entrepreneurship, wages, and leadership. Addressing them requires integrated policies and programs that target these multifaceted challenges.

3. Breaking Barriers: Key Challenges and Opportunities

3.1 Education and Skill Development

Access to quality education and skills training is a critical foundation for enabling women to participate effectively in high-growth economic sectors. Education not only provides the knowledge and technical competencies needed to compete in today's labor markets but also fosters confidence, critical thinking, and problem-solving skills essential for leadership and innovation.

Particularly important is the focus on science, technology, engineering, and mathematics (STEM) education, as these fields underpin many of the fastest-growing industries globally, including information technology, renewable energy, biotechnology, and advanced manufacturing. Despite progress, women and girls remain underrepresented in STEM education and careers due to persistent stereotypes, lack of role models, and educational biases.

Moreover, digital literacy and vocational training tailored to evolving market demands empower women to access emerging opportunities in the digital economy and the gig sector. Lifelong learning initiatives and reskilling programs are also vital for women whose jobs are affected by automation and technological change.

Beyond formal education, soft skills such as communication, leadership, and financial literacy are equally important for enabling women to seize entrepreneurial and managerial roles. Ensuring that educational systems are inclusive, gender-sensitive, and equipped to support girls through secondary and tertiary levels is crucial to closing gender gaps and unlocking women's full economic potential.

3.2 Access to Finance

Access to finance remains one of the most significant hurdles for women entrepreneurs and women-led businesses, limiting their ability to start, sustain, and scale their ventures. Women often face structural barriers such as lack of collateral—especially property or land ownership—which financial institutions typically require for loans. Additionally, many women have limited or no formal credit history, which restricts their eligibility for conventional credit products.

Gender bias within financial institutions can further exacerbate these challenges, with women frequently receiving less favorable loan terms, higher interest rates, or outright rejection despite strong business proposals. These biases may stem from outdated assumptions about women's creditworthiness or business capabilities.

To overcome these barriers, gender-sensitive financial products and services have been developed. These include microfinance loans with flexible collateral requirements, group lending models that leverage social capital, and innovative fintech solutions such as mobile banking and digital credit scoring that better capture women's financial behaviors and risks. Financial literacy programs tailored to women entrepreneurs also play a crucial role by enhancing their ability to manage finances, build credit, and negotiate with lenders.

Improving women's access to diverse financial tools not only supports individual business growth but also has multiplier effects on household welfare, job creation, and broader economic development.

3.3 Entrepreneurship and Business Growth

Scaling women-owned businesses is critical for driving economic growth, job creation, and innovation. However, women entrepreneurs often face unique challenges that hinder their ability to grow beyond the startup phase. To overcome these obstacles, a comprehensive support system is essential—one that encompasses mentorship, access to markets, and a conducive regulatory environment.

- **Mentorship and Networking:** Access to experienced mentors and professional networks provides women entrepreneurs with invaluable guidance, business acumen, and connections that open doors to new opportunities. Mentorship helps build confidence, develop leadership skills, and navigate complex business environments.
- **Market Access:** Women-owned businesses frequently encounter barriers to entering and expanding in local, national, and global markets. Limited networks, gender biases in procurement processes, and lack of market information restrict their reach. Facilitating access through inclusive procurement policies, trade fairs, and digital marketplaces can significantly enhance their growth prospects.
- **Enabling Regulatory Environments:** Regulatory frameworks that are transparent, gender-responsive, and reduce bureaucratic burdens are vital for women entrepreneurs. Simplified business registration, tax incentives, and protections against discriminatory practices create an enabling environment that encourages women to formalize and scale their enterprises.

Additionally, capacity-building programs focused on financial management, innovation, and digital tools empower women to enhance competitiveness and sustainability. When these support mechanisms are combined, women entrepreneurs can overcome traditional barriers, unlock growth potential, and become influential drivers of economic transformation.

3.4 Leadership and Representation

Women's leadership in both the public and private sectors is a powerful catalyst for inclusive economic growth and equitable development. Diverse leadership teams foster innovation, improve decision-making, and ensure that policies and business strategies reflect the needs of all segments of society. Evidence shows that organizations with greater gender diversity in leadership roles tend to perform better financially and are more resilient in times of crisis.

However, women remain underrepresented in senior management and executive positions globally. This disparity is largely due to entrenched discrimination, conscious and unconscious biases, and systemic barriers that limit women's access to leadership pipelines. These include unequal access to mentorship, networking opportunities, and leadership development programs, as well as workplace cultures that may be unwelcoming or hostile to women.

Moreover, structural challenges such as inflexible work arrangements, lack of family-friendly policies, and societal expectations around caregiving disproportionately affect women's career progression. The absence of transparent promotion criteria and gender-equity targets further perpetuates the leadership gap.

Addressing these challenges requires deliberate strategies such as establishing mentorship and sponsorship programs, implementing gender quotas or targets, promoting inclusive organizational cultures, and adopting policies that support work-life balance. By investing in women's leadership development and removing structural barriers, societies can harness the full potential of women leaders to drive sustainable and inclusive economic growth.

4. Strategies for Promoting Women's Growth

4.1 Policy Interventions

Effective policy interventions are fundamental to creating an enabling environment where women can fully participate and lead in economic growth. Governments play a critical role by enacting gender-responsive policies that address the systemic barriers women face and promote equality across all economic sectors.

The Rise of Women in Leadership

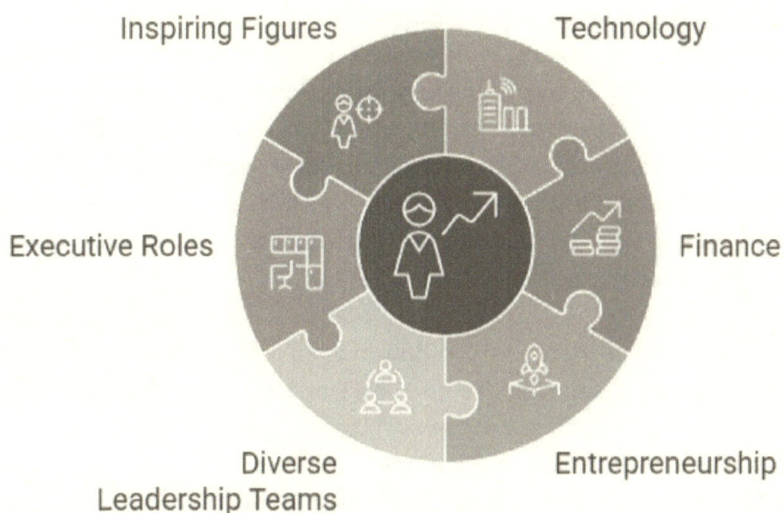

The Rise of Women in Leadership

Key policy areas include:

- **Labor Laws:** Enacting and enforcing labor laws that ensure equal pay for equal work, prohibit workplace discrimination and harassment, and guarantee maternity and parental leave are essential steps toward gender equality in the workforce. Policies that promote flexible working arrangements help women balance professional and caregiving responsibilities.

- **Social Protections:** Expanding social safety nets such as healthcare, unemployment benefits, and childcare support reduces the economic vulnerabilities that disproportionately affect women. These protections enable women to engage more confidently in formal employment and entrepreneurship.

- **Investment in Women's Economic Sectors:** Targeted public investments in sectors where women are heavily employed—such as healthcare, education, and agriculture—can drive job creation and improve working conditions. Additionally, supporting women-led enterprises through grants, subsidies, or procurement preferences strengthens their competitiveness.
- **Legal Reforms:** Removing discriminatory laws related to property rights, inheritance, and business ownership is vital for women's economic autonomy. Simplifying regulatory procedures encourages women to formalize their businesses, gaining access to credit and legal protections.
- **Data and Monitoring:** Establishing gender-disaggregated data systems and monitoring frameworks helps policymakers assess progress, identify gaps, and design evidence-based interventions that address women's specific economic needs.

By integrating gender considerations into all aspects of economic policy, governments can dismantle structural barriers and foster inclusive growth that benefits women and society as a whole.

4.2 Financial Inclusion Innovations

Innovative financial technologies (fintech), microfinance, and digital banking have emerged as powerful tools to overcome traditional barriers that limit women's access to capital and financial services. These innovations are reshaping the financial landscape by providing more inclusive, affordable, and accessible options tailored to women's unique needs.

- **Fintech Solutions:** Mobile money platforms, peer-to-peer lending, and digital wallets enable women—especially in remote or underserved areas—to conduct transactions, save, and borrow without requiring physical bank branches or extensive documentation. Fintech also leverages alternative data for credit scoring, such as mobile phone usage or social behavior, which can help women with limited credit history qualify for loans.
- **Microfinance:** Microfinance institutions have a long history of empowering women entrepreneurs by offering small loans, savings, and insurance products designed to meet their specific circumstances. Group lending models foster community support and accountability, making it

easier for women to access funds and build credit.

- **Digital Banking:** The growth of digital-only banks and apps reduces bureaucratic hurdles and transaction costs, making financial services more user-friendly and accessible. Many digital banks offer educational resources and budgeting tools that enhance women's financial literacy and management skills.
- Together, these innovations not only improve access to capital but also enhance financial inclusion by providing women with the tools to manage their money securely and independently. Scaling these solutions, along with supportive regulatory frameworks and gender-sensitive design, is crucial to closing the gender finance gap and enabling women's economic growth.

4.3 Education and Training Programs

Expanding access to education and targeted training programs is essential for enhancing women's employability, particularly in emerging and high-growth industries. As the global economy increasingly depends on technology, innovation, and specialized skills, providing women with the necessary education and vocational training ensures they are not left behind.

- **STEM Education:** Science, Technology, Engineering, and Mathematics (STEM) fields are critical drivers of economic growth and innovation. However, women remain significantly underrepresented in these areas due to cultural stereotypes, lack of female role models, and limited encouragement in early education. Increasing investment in girls' STEM education—from primary school through higher education—combined with mentorship and scholarship programs, can help close this gap and prepare women for careers in cutting-edge sectors such as artificial intelligence, biotechnology, and renewable energy.
- **Vocational Training:** Practical, skills-based training aligned with market needs equips women with competencies that enhance their job prospects and income-earning potential. Vocational programs focused on digital skills, trades, and entrepreneurship provide women with alternatives to traditional academic pathways and foster economic independence.
- **Lifelong Learning and Reskilling:** As industries evolve rapidly due to technological advancements and globalization, ongoing education and

reskilling programs are crucial. These initiatives help women adapt to changing labor market demands, especially those whose jobs are vulnerable to automation.

- **Inclusive Curriculum and Delivery**: Education and training programs must be designed to be gender-sensitive, accessible, and flexible, accommodating women's schedules and addressing barriers such as caregiving responsibilities. Online platforms and community-based training can expand reach and participation.

By investing in comprehensive education and training programs, policymakers and stakeholders can empower women with the skills needed to participate meaningfully in economic growth and leadership in emerging sectors.

4.4 Corporate and Social Initiatives

Private sector engagement and social initiatives play a pivotal role in advancing women's economic growth by fostering environments that prioritize diversity, equity, and inclusion (DEI). As businesses recognize the competitive and ethical benefits of gender diversity, many are implementing strategies to create pathways for women's advancement across all levels of the organization.

- **Corporate Commitments**: Leading companies are setting explicit gender diversity targets, including increasing the representation of women in leadership roles, boards, and technical positions. These commitments are often accompanied by transparent reporting, accountability mechanisms, and inclusive hiring practices that actively seek to eliminate biases.
- **Workplace Policies**: Inclusive workplace policies—such as flexible working hours, parental leave, childcare support, and anti-harassment measures—help retain and promote women by addressing the unique challenges they face in balancing work and family responsibilities. Such policies create a supportive culture that values and respects women's contributions.
- **Employee Resource Groups and Mentorship**: Many organizations facilitate women's networks and mentorship programs that provide professional development, peer support, and leadership coaching. These initiatives help women build confidence, skills, and connections necessary for career advancement.

- **Social Impact Initiatives:** Beyond internal policies, companies increasingly invest in social programs that empower women entrepreneurs and communities through capacity-building, funding, and partnerships. Corporate social responsibility efforts focused on gender equity can amplify women's economic participation at the grassroots level.
- **Collaborative Ecosystems:** Partnerships among corporations, governments, NGOs, and academia foster innovative approaches and scale successful models for women's empowerment. Such ecosystems facilitate knowledge sharing, resource mobilization, and policy advocacy.

By embedding DEI into corporate strategy and culture, the private sector can be a powerful engine for breaking down barriers and unlocking women's full economic potential.

5. Case Studies: Success Stories from Around the World

5.1 Rwanda's Gender-Inclusive Economic Policies

Rwanda stands out as a global leader in promoting gender equality through comprehensive and deliberate economic policies. Following the 1994 genocide, Rwanda integrated gender considerations into its national development agenda, resulting in one of the highest rates of female parliamentary representation worldwide. The government has enacted laws ensuring women's property rights, access to finance, and participation in entrepreneurship. Rwanda's Vision 2020 and subsequent development plans emphasize women's economic empowerment as key to sustainable growth. Programs such as the Women Guarantee Fund provide affordable loans to women entrepreneurs, facilitating business growth and financial independence. These efforts have contributed to increasing women's participation in agriculture, trade, and formal sectors, showcasing how policy commitment can transform women's economic status.

5.2 Microfinance and Women's Entrepreneurship in Bangladesh

Bangladesh is renowned for pioneering microfinance initiatives that have empowered millions of women, particularly through organizations like the Grameen Bank and BRAC. By providing small, collateral-free loans to women in rural and urban areas, microfinance programs have enabled them to start and expand businesses, improve household incomes, and gain financial autonomy. Group lending models foster social cohesion and accountability, helping borrowers overcome traditional lending barriers. This approach has not only lifted many women out of poverty but also catalyzed broader community development. The success of microfinance in Bangladesh illustrates the transformative potential of financial inclusion tailored to women's realities.

5.3 Corporate Leadership Programs for Women in Scandinavia

Scandinavian countries, including Sweden, Norway, and Denmark, are internationally recognized for their progressive gender equality policies and corporate leadership initiatives. These nations have implemented gender quotas on corporate boards, robust parental leave policies, and support systems that promote work-life balance. Leadership development programs tailored for women—such as mentorship, executive training, and networking forums—have significantly increased female representation in senior management roles. The private sector's commitment to diversity, combined with strong government frameworks, has created an enabling environment where women thrive as business leaders and innovators, driving inclusive economic growth.

5.4 Digital Platforms Empowering Women in Sub-Saharan Africa

In sub-Saharan Africa, digital technology has become a vital tool for empowering women entrepreneurs and workers. Platforms like M-Pesa in Kenya revolutionized mobile money, enabling women without access to traditional banking to save, transfer money, and obtain credit via mobile phones. E-commerce platforms and digital marketplaces allow women artisans and small business owners to reach broader markets beyond local limitations. Additionally, online training and mentorship programs provide skills development and networking opportunities, bridging geographic and social divides. These digital innovations are enhancing women's economic participation and resilience in a region where formal financial and business infrastructure is often limited.

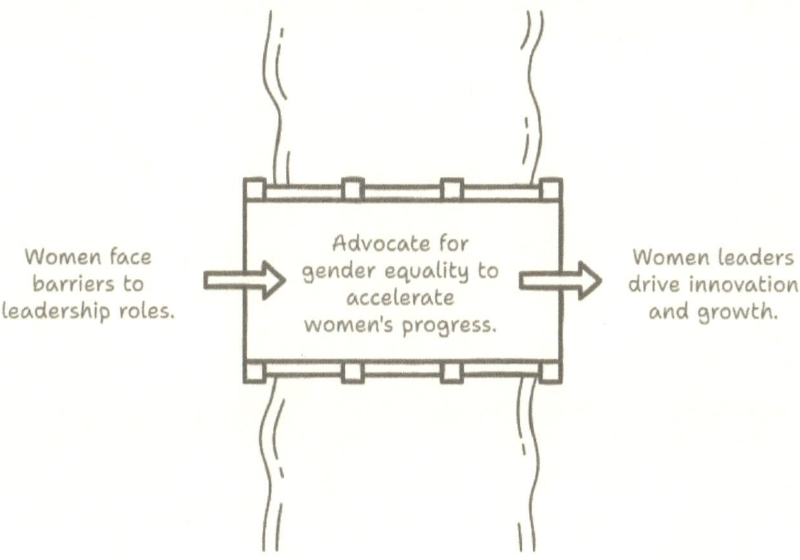

Empowering Women Leaders for Accelerated Growth

6. Conclusion

Unlocking women's potential in economic growth is not only a matter of equity but a strategic imperative for sustainable development. Breaking barriers requires coordinated efforts across education, finance, policy, and culture. With deliberate action, women can be powerful catalysts for inclusive and resilient economies.

References

1. Aterido, R., Beck, T., & Iacovone, L. (2013). Access to Finance in Sub-Saharan Africa: Is There a Gender Gap? World Development, 47, 102-120. https://doi.org/10.1016/j.worlddev.2013.02.013

2. Charmes, J. (2019). Unpaid Care Work: The Missing Link in the Analysis of Gender Gaps in Labor Outcomes. International Labour Review, 158(2), 345-365. https://doi.org/10.1111/ilr.12131

3. *Deere, C. D., & Doss, C. (2006). The Gender Asset Gap: What Do We Know and Why Does It Matter? Feminist Economics, 12(1-2), 1-50. https://doi.org/10.1080/13545700500508069*

4. *Elson, D. (2017). Gender Equality and Economic Growth: Is There a Win-Win? Feminist Economics, 23(1), 1-35. https://doi.org/10.1080/13545701.2016.1216850*

5. *Kabeer, N. (2012). Women's Economic Empowerment and Inclusive Growth: Labour Markets and Enterprise Development. International Development Research Centre.*

6. *McKinsey Global Institute. (2015). The Power of Parity: How Advancing Women's Equality Can Add $12 Trillion to Global Growth. McKinsey & Company. https://www.mckinsey.com/featured-insights/employment-and-growth/the-power-of-parity-advancing-womens-equality-can-add-12-trillion-to-global-growth*

7. *Nussbaum, M. C. (2000). Women and Human Development: The Capabilities Approach. Cambridge University Press.*

8. *OECD. (2019). Closing the Gender Gap: Act Now. OECD Publishing. https://doi.org/10.1787/9789264311318-en*

9. *PwC. (2021). Women in Work Index 2021. PricewaterhouseCoopers. https://www.pwc.com/gx/en/about/diversity/women-in-work.html*

10. *World Bank. (2018). Women, Business and the Law 2018. Washington, DC: World Bank Group. https://openknowledge.worldbank.org/handle/10986/29498*

11. *World Economic Forum. (2023). Global Gender Gap Report 2023. https://www.weforum.org/reports/global-gender-gap-report-2023*

12. *Yadav, P., & Kesarwani, R. (2020). Microfinance and Women Empowerment: Evidence from India. Journal of Rural Development, 39(1), 113-126.*

CHAPTER TWENTY

The Role of Self-Help Groups (SHGs) in Promoting Women Entrepreneurship in Bihar

Author: Pushkar Kumar Singh, Research scholar at Jai Prakash University, Chhapra, Bihar

Abstract

Self-Help Groups (SHGs) have become a cornerstone of women's economic empowerment in Bihar, India, facilitating access to finance, skill development, and market linkages for aspiring women entrepreneurs. This chapter explores how SHGs contribute to promoting women entrepreneurship in Bihar by addressing financial exclusion, fostering collective action, and enhancing social capital. It examines government initiatives, challenges faced by SHGs, and the impact on women's socio-economic status. The chapter concludes with policy recommendations to strengthen SHG networks and scale women-led enterprises in Bihar.

Keywords: Self-Help Groups, Women Entrepreneurship, Bihar, Microfinance, Economic Empowerment, Collective Action

1. Introduction

Bihar, one of India's most populous states, is predominantly rural, with over 80% of its population residing in villages. Despite rich cultural heritage and agricultural potential, the state faces persistent economic challenges including low industrialization, widespread poverty, low literacy rates, and limited infrastructure. These structural constraints have historically hindered economic opportunities for all, but especially for women, who often face additional barriers due to entrenched social norms and gender inequalities.

In this context, Self-Help Groups (SHGs) have emerged as a transformative grassroots mechanism to promote women's economic participation and empowerment. Originating as informal collectives of women who pool savings and extend credit among themselves, SHGs in Bihar have evolved into vital platforms that enable women to overcome financial exclusion, build social capital, and develop entrepreneurial skills.

By facilitating access to credit and financial services in areas where formal banking infrastructure is limited, SHGs empower women to start and grow small businesses, engage in income-generating activities, and contribute to their household and community economies. Beyond economic benefits, SHGs foster mutual support, collective decision-making, and greater confidence among women, challenging traditional gender roles and enhancing their social status.

This chapter explores how SHGs in Bihar have played a crucial role in advancing women entrepreneurship, the challenges they face, and the policy interventions necessary to amplify their impact for inclusive and sustainable economic growth.

2. Context: Women Entrepreneurship in Bihar

Women in Bihar have traditionally faced significant social and economic constraints that have limited their participation in formal economic activities. Deep-rooted patriarchal norms often restrict women's mobility and decision-making power, confining many to household and unpaid care work. Additionally, lower levels of education and skill development among women, compared to men, have further limited their access to entrepreneurial opportunities. Early marriage, limited exposure to markets, and restricted control over family resources also hamper their ability to start or scale businesses.

Despite these challenges, there is a growing recognition among women in Bihar of the need for economic self-reliance and entrepreneurship. Factors such as increased awareness through government schemes, NGO interventions, and exposure to microfinance have encouraged more women to pursue income-generating activities. Women are now increasingly engaging in diverse sectors including agriculture, livestock rearing, handicrafts, food processing, and small-scale retail.

However, critical barriers remain. Access to formal finance is limited due to lack of collateral, credit history, and gender biases in lending institutions. Many women also lack the necessary business skills, market knowledge, and networks to sustain and grow their ventures. This is compounded by inadequate infrastructure, poor market linkages, and often a lack of supportive legal and policy frameworks tailored to women entrepreneurs.

In this challenging environment, Self-Help Groups (SHGs) have emerged as an effective grassroots platform that addresses multiple constraints simultaneously. By pooling financial resources and collective knowledge, SHGs enable women to access credit, receive training, and gain peer support. This collective approach helps women overcome individual limitations, build confidence, and access markets more effectively. As a result, SHGs have become a catalyst for promoting women entrepreneurship in Bihar, providing a pathway for greater economic participation and empowerment.

3. Formation and Functioning of SHGs

Self-Help Groups (SHGs) in Bihar typically consist of 10 to 20 women members, often drawn from similar socio-economic and geographic backgrounds. This homogeneity helps build trust and mutual understanding among members, which is fundamental for the effective functioning of the group. The SHG model is based on principles of collective savings, mutual accountability, and peer support, which empower women to take charge of their financial and entrepreneurial journeys.

The formation of SHGs usually begins with community mobilization, often facilitated by government agencies, non-governmental organizations (NGOs), or local leaders who identify motivated women and encourage group formation. Initial meetings focus on establishing group rules, roles, and the frequency of gatherings. Emphasis is placed on transparency, democratic decision-making, and regular savings contributions, which are essential to building group cohesion and financial discipline.

A core activity of SHGs is the pooling of savings, where each member contributes a fixed amount regularly. These pooled funds create an internal lending mechanism, enabling members to access small loans without the need for collateral or formal credit history. Loans are typically used for income-generating activities, household needs, or emergencies. The revolving nature of the fund fosters financial independence and builds creditworthiness among women.

Beyond savings and credit, SHGs in Bihar often register under government initiatives such as the National Rural Livelihood Mission (NRLM). This affiliation provides SHGs with access to formal banking services, subsidies, training programs, and linkages to government welfare schemes. The NRLM facilitates bank linkages that allow SHGs to secure larger loans, access financial products, and participate in broader economic activities.

Capacity-building is another critical aspect of SHG functioning. Members receive training on financial literacy, bookkeeping, entrepreneurial skills, and leadership development. These programs are designed to enhance the group's ability to manage finances effectively, make informed business decisions, and improve their overall economic prospects.

In summary, the success of SHGs in Bihar hinges on strong group dynamics, regular savings and lending practices, institutional support from government programs, and continuous capacity-building efforts. These elements combine to create a sustainable platform for women to overcome financial exclusion and engage in entrepreneurship.

Key functions include:

Micro-savings and Credit Access: A foundational pillar of Self-Help Groups (SHGs) is their micro-savings and credit mechanism, which plays a critical role in empowering women financially. Each member of an SHG contributes a small, regular amount of money to a common fund, often referred to as the group's savings pool. These contributions, though modest individually, accumulate to create a substantial fund that is owned collectively by the group.

This micro-savings practice instills financial discipline among women, many of whom previously lacked the habit or opportunity to save money formally. Regular saving fosters a sense of ownership and responsibility, reinforcing trust within the group and encouraging members to participate actively.

The pooled savings are then used to provide internal loans to group members who need capital for income-generating activities, household expenses, or emergencies. Unlike formal bank loans, these internal loans do not require collateral or credit history, making them highly accessible to women who are often excluded from traditional financial systems.

Loan terms, interest rates, and repayment schedules are decided democratically by the SHG members, ensuring transparency and fairness. The revolving loan fund is replenished as members repay their loans, enabling continuous access to credit within the group.

This internal credit mechanism addresses critical barriers faced by women entrepreneurs, such as lack of collateral, high-interest rates from informal lenders, and bureaucratic hurdles in banks. By providing timely and affordable credit, SHGs enable women to start or expand small businesses, invest in productive assets, and improve household welfare.

Furthermore, the experience of borrowing and repaying within the SHG helps women build financial credibility and confidence. Over time, successful SHGs can link with formal banking institutions to access larger loans and government subsidies, amplifying their economic impact.

In summary, micro-savings and credit access through SHGs offer a practical, community-driven solution to financial exclusion, empowering women to take control of their economic futures.

Financial Linkages: Facilitating access to bank credit and government subsidies. One of the transformative roles of Self-Help Groups (SHGs) in Bihar is their ability to bridge the gap between rural women entrepreneurs and formal financial institutions. While internal savings and lending provide immediate financial support, SHGs often serve as intermediaries that facilitate access to larger-scale bank credit and government subsidies, which are crucial for scaling up entrepreneurial ventures.

The linkage process typically begins when an SHG, having demonstrated financial discipline and effective management of its internal funds, approaches banks for formal credit. Recognized under schemes like the National Rural Livelihood Mission (NRLM), SHGs are often registered and graded based on their financial health and governance practices. Banks are more willing to extend loans to SHGs because the collective liability model reduces the risk of default compared to individual lending.

By obtaining bank credit, SHGs gain access to larger sums of capital than their pooled savings alone can provide. This capital enables women entrepreneurs to invest in more substantial business opportunities, purchase equipment, expand production, or diversify their income sources. Moreover, access to formal finance typically comes at lower interest rates than informal lenders, making borrowing more affordable and sustainable.

In addition to bank credit, SHGs play a critical role in connecting women to various government subsidies and welfare schemes designed to promote entrepreneurship and livelihood development. These may include grants for skill training, subsidies on inputs like seeds or machinery, and benefits under schemes for women's empowerment and rural development.

Government programs often require a formal organizational structure or collective entity to disburse funds effectively and monitor outcomes. SHGs provide this institutional framework, making women eligible to receive and manage government resources transparently and efficiently. The linkage thus ensures that benefits reach the intended beneficiaries without leakage or delay.

Through these financial linkages, SHGs not only enhance women's access to capital but also integrate them into the broader economic system, enabling participation in mainstream development processes. This formal engagement helps build credit histories for SHGs and their members, further improving their financial inclusion and sustainability.

In summary, financial linkages act as a critical enabler for SHGs by connecting grassroots women entrepreneurs with formal banking services and government support, thereby expanding their capacity for economic growth and empowerment.

Capacity Building: Capacity building is a vital component of Self-Help Groups' (SHGs) role in empowering women entrepreneurs in Bihar. Beyond facilitating savings and credit, SHGs actively engage in enhancing the knowledge, skills, and competencies of their members through targeted training programs. These initiatives aim to equip women with the tools necessary to start, manage, and grow their businesses sustainably.

- **Entrepreneurship Training:** SHGs often organize workshops and training sessions that introduce women to fundamental concepts of entrepreneurship, including business planning, market analysis, cost management, and customer relations. These sessions help women understand how to identify viable business opportunities, develop business models, and navigate challenges commonly faced by small enterprises. Learning entrepreneurial skills increases women's confidence and encourages innovation within their ventures.
- **Financial Literacy:** Understanding financial management is crucial for the success of any business. SHGs provide training on budgeting, record-keeping, bookkeeping, loan management, and savings practices. Women learn how to track income and expenses, prepare simple financial statements, and make informed decisions about investment and borrowing. Financial literacy also enables women to better engage with formal financial institutions and comply with loan requirements, enhancing their credibility as entrepreneurs.
- **Vocational Skills Training:** To diversify income sources and improve product quality, SHGs facilitate vocational training tailored to local economic contexts. This can include skills development in areas such as tailoring, handicrafts, food processing, agriculture-related activities, and digital literacy. Vocational training not only increases women's

employability but also opens up opportunities for entrepreneurship in specialized sectors, contributing to higher incomes and economic resilience.

Capacity building efforts are often conducted in collaboration with government agencies, NGOs, and technical institutes, leveraging expertise and resources to deliver comprehensive and context-specific training. The participatory and peer-learning environment of SHGs fosters a supportive space where women can practice new skills, share experiences, and build networks.

In summary, capacity building through entrepreneurship, financial literacy, and vocational training equips SHG members with the essential skills to enhance their business capabilities, improve financial management, and adapt to evolving market demands—thereby strengthening women's economic empowerment and sustainability.

4. Impact on Women Entrepreneurship

SHGs have catalyzed the growth of diverse women-led enterprises in sectors such as agriculture, dairy, handicrafts, food processing, and retail. By lowering financial and informational barriers, SHGs empower women to initiate and sustain businesses, leading to increased household incomes and social status.

5. Challenges and Limitations

While Self-Help Groups (SHGs) have significantly advanced women's entrepreneurship in Bihar, they continue to encounter several challenges and limitations that hinder their full potential. Understanding these obstacles is crucial for designing effective interventions and policies to strengthen SHG-led economic empowerment.

Despite successes, SHGs in Bihar face challenges including:

Limited access to formal credit beyond small loans: Although SHGs successfully mobilize internal savings and access small-scale bank loans, many struggle to secure larger or long-term credit necessary for business expansion. Formal financial institutions often hesitate to provide substantial loans due to perceived risks, lack of collateral, and limited credit histories of SHGs and their members. This credit constraint restricts women entrepreneurs from scaling operations or investing in higher-value ventures.

Inadequate market linkages and infrastructure: Many women-led enterprises supported by SHGs operate in isolated rural areas with poor connectivity, limited transportation, and insufficient market information. These infrastructural deficits reduce access to larger markets, limit customer reach, and increase transaction costs. Furthermore, weak linkages with buyers, suppliers, and business networks hamper the ability of women entrepreneurs to negotiate better prices or diversify their products.

Persistent gender norms restricting women's mobility and decision-making: Deep-rooted patriarchal attitudes and social norms continue to curtail women's mobility and participation in economic activities. Many women face restrictions on traveling outside their villages or engaging freely in public economic spaces. Decision-making authority over financial resources often remains with male family members, limiting women's autonomy to invest in or manage businesses independently. Such norms also affect women's participation in SHG leadership and training opportunities.

Capacity constraints in group management and business development: Effective SHG functioning requires strong organizational, financial, and managerial skills. However, many SHGs face challenges related to limited literacy levels, inadequate bookkeeping practices, and poor governance structures. Similarly, members often lack advanced entrepreneurial skills and access to professional business development services. These capacity gaps reduce the ability of SHGs to operate efficiently, access higher-value markets, or innovate.

6. Government and Institutional Support

The Government of Bihar, recognizing the transformative potential of Self-Help Groups (SHGs) in promoting women's entrepreneurship and economic empowerment, has undertaken a range of initiatives to support and scale these grassroots institutions. In collaboration with national programs such as the National Rural Livelihood Mission (NRLM)—also known as Ajeevika Mission—and a host of non-governmental organizations (NGOs), the state has created an enabling environment for SHG formation, capacity building, and financial inclusion.

- **Promotion of SHG Formation and Institutional Strengthening:**
  Government agencies facilitate the mobilization and registration of SHGs across rural and semi-urban areas in Bihar. Through village-level workers and community facilitators, women are encouraged to come together, form groups, and build savings habits. The government also promotes federations or clusters of SHGs to improve governance,

bargaining power, and access to resources at higher levels.

- **Financial Inclusion Drives:**
  The Government of Bihar actively works to link SHGs with formal financial institutions such as banks and microfinance institutions. Special efforts are made to open bank accounts for SHGs and facilitate bank credit, often with subsidized interest rates or guarantees under government schemes. Financial inclusion drives also include digital literacy programs to help women use mobile banking and digital payment platforms, expanding their access to financial services.

- **Training and Capacity Building Programs:**
  In partnership with NGOs and technical agencies, the government organizes regular training programs covering entrepreneurship development, financial literacy, vocational skills, and group management. These capacity-building efforts aim to enhance SHG members' business acumen, financial management capabilities, and leadership skills. Additionally, the government promotes awareness about existing welfare schemes and opportunities for women entrepreneurs.

- **Schemes Encouraging Women's Entrepreneurship:**
  Several state and central government schemes specifically target women entrepreneurs through SHGs. These include subsidies on capital investments, skill development grants, market access facilitation, and support for product branding and packaging. The government also encourages women's participation in sectors such as agriculture, dairy, handicrafts, and small-scale manufacturing through targeted interventions.

- **Partnerships with NGOs and Private Sector:**
  NGOs play a critical role as facilitators and trainers, often bridging the gap between government programs and grassroots communities. Some private sector initiatives also collaborate with SHGs for corporate social responsibility (CSR) projects, providing technical assistance, market linkages, and incubation support.

- **Monitoring and Evaluation:**
  To ensure effective implementation, the government has established monitoring frameworks to track SHG performance, financial health, and socio-economic impact. Data-driven approaches help refine policies, allocate resources efficiently, and scale successful models.

7. Policy Recommendations

To maximize the impact of Self-Help Groups (SHGs) in fostering women's entrepreneurship and economic empowerment in Bihar, a comprehensive and multi-dimensional policy approach is essential. The following recommendations outline key measures to address existing challenges and build a sustainable, enabling environment:

- **1. Strengthening Credit Access through Tailored Financial Products:** Financial institutions should design and offer credit products that are specifically tailored to the needs of women entrepreneurs within SHGs. This includes flexible loan sizes, collateral-free loans, and longer repayment periods aligned with the cash flow patterns of small-scale enterprises. Introducing credit guarantee schemes and interest subsidies can further reduce borrowing costs and risks. Additionally, promoting digital credit platforms and mobile banking can facilitate easier loan disbursement and monitoring.

- **2. Enhancing Market Linkages via Digital Platforms and Cooperative Models:** To overcome the barriers of poor infrastructure and limited market access, the government and development partners should support SHGs in leveraging digital technologies for market outreach. Creating e-commerce platforms dedicated to SHG products and training women on digital marketing can open up new customer bases. Encouraging SHG federations or cooperatives can also enhance collective bargaining power, enable bulk procurement of raw materials, and improve access to larger and more profitable markets.

- **3. Expanding Capacity-Building Programs Focused on Business Management:** Training initiatives should be scaled up with a focus on practical business skills, including financial literacy, record-keeping, marketing, and use of technology. Customized modules that address sector-specific needs and challenges faced by women entrepreneurs can enhance relevance and effectiveness. Additionally, mentoring and peer learning networks can provide ongoing support and motivation.

- **4. Addressing Socio-Cultural Barriers through Awareness Campaigns:** Sustained efforts are needed to challenge and change entrenched gender norms that limit women's mobility, decision-making, and economic participation. Community-based awareness campaigns involving local leaders, men, and youth can foster more supportive attitudes toward women's entrepreneurship. Gender sensitization programs integrated into school curricula and public forums can contribute to long-term cultural shifts.

- **5. Strengthening Institutional Support and Monitoring:**
Enhancing coordination between government departments, NGOs, financial institutions, and private sector partners is vital for cohesive program delivery. Establishing robust monitoring and evaluation frameworks will ensure transparency, accountability, and continuous improvement of SHG initiatives.

- **6. Facilitating Access to Infrastructure and Technology:**
Investments in rural infrastructure such as roads, electricity, internet connectivity, and marketplaces are essential to support women-led enterprises. Promoting access to affordable technology and mechanization can improve productivity and reduce drudgery.

8. Conclusion

SHGs represent a vital pathway for empowering women entrepreneurs in Bihar, fostering economic independence and social transformation. With sustained policy support and innovative interventions, SHGs can significantly contribute to inclusive economic growth and gender equality in the region.

References

1. *Agarwal, B. (2010). Gender and Green Governance: The Political Economy of Women's Presence Within and Beyond Community Forestry. Oxford University Press.*

2. *Bhattacharyya, R. (2015). Self Help Groups and Women's Empowerment: Evidence from Rural Bihar. Journal of Rural Development, 34(1), 97–115.*

3. *Government of India. (2011). National Rural Livelihood Mission (NRLM): Strategy and Guidelines. Ministry of Rural Development. https://nrlm.gov.in*

4. *Kabeer, N. (2005). Gender Equality and Women's Empowerment: A Critical Analysis of the Third Millennium Development Goal 1. Gender & Development, 13(1), 13–24.*

5. *Mahajan, V., & Venkatesh, M. (2019). Microfinance and Women Empowerment: A Study of Self-Help Groups in Bihar. International Journal of Social Economics, 46(2), 253–266.*

6. *Ministry of Women and Child Development. (2020). Annual Report 2019-2020. Government of India.*

7. *National Bank for Agriculture and Rural Development (NABARD). (2018). Report on Status of Microfinance in India. Mumbai: NABARD.*

8. *Rai, P., & Singh, S. (2021). Challenges Faced by Women Entrepreneurs in Bihar: A Study on Self Help Groups. International Journal of Management Studies, 8(3), 112–125.*

9. *Singh, R., & Sharma, A. (2017). Financial Inclusion and Empowerment of Rural Women through Self-Help Groups in Bihar. Indian Journal of Economics and Development, 13(3), 407–414.*

10. *World Bank. (2014). Empowering Women Entrepreneurs through Access to Finance and Markets. Washington, DC: World Bank Publications.*

11. *Zeller, M., & Sharma, M. (2000). Promoting Women's Self-Help Groups in India: Implications for Access to Credit and Income Generation. Food Consumption and Nutrition Division, International Food Policy Research Institute.*

CHAPTER TWENTY-ONE

Investigations into Hydrodynamic and Magnetohydrodynamic Convective Flows

Author: *Vinay Shankar Dubey, Research Scholar at Nehru Gram Bharati University, Prayagraj*

Abstract

This chapter explores recent advancements in the study of hydrodynamic and magnetohydrodynamic (MHD) convective flows. Convection plays a vital role in various natural and engineering systems, influencing heat transfer, fluid mixing, and magnetic field dynamics. We review fundamental concepts, governing equations, and key dimensionless parameters. The chapter discusses both experimental and theoretical investigations, including stability analyses, nonlinear behavior, and flow patterns under the influence of magnetic fields. Applications in geophysics, astrophysics, and industrial processes are highlighted, alongside challenges and future research directions.

Keywords: Hydrodynamics, Magnetohydrodynamics, Convection, Stability analysis, Heat transfer, Magnetic fields, Fluid dynamics, Nonlinear flow.

1. Introduction

Convective flows arise due to buoyancy forces induced by temperature gradients in fluid media. When electrically conducting fluids are subjected to magnetic fields, magnetohydrodynamic (MHD) effects significantly alter flow characteristics and heat transfer processes. Understanding these phenomena is crucial for applications ranging from geophysical flows in the

Earth's outer core to cooling in nuclear reactors. Convection is a primary mechanism for heat and mass transfer in fluids subjected to temperature gradients. In many natural and engineering contexts, such as the Earth's outer core, stellar interiors, and liquid metal cooling systems, the fluid is electrically conducting and subjected to magnetic fields. These systems are governed by the principles of magnetohydrodynamics (MHD), where the interaction between magnetic fields and fluid motion leads to complex flow behavior.

This paper focuses on the theoretical aspects of convective instability and flow dynamics in both hydrodynamic and MHD frameworks. We aim to establish a fundamental understanding of how magnetic fields modify the onset and nature of convective flows.

2. Governing Equations and Dimensionless Parameters

2.1 Hydrodynamic Convection

The motion of a viscous incompressible fluid heated from below can be described by the Navier-Stokes equations coupled with the heat equation:

$$\frac{\partial \mathbf{u}}{\partial t} + (\mathbf{u} \cdot \nabla)\mathbf{u} = -\frac{1}{\rho}\nabla p + \nu\nabla^2\mathbf{u} + \mathbf{g}\beta(T - T_0)$$

$$\frac{\partial T}{\partial t} + (\mathbf{u} \cdot \nabla)T = \kappa\nabla^2 T$$

where $\mathbf{u}$ is the velocity field, p is pressure, ρ density, ν kinematic viscosity, $\mathbf{g}$ gravity, β thermal expansion coefficient, T temperature, and κ thermal diffusivity.

2.2 Magnetohydrodynamic Convection

For electrically conducting fluids, the MHD equations couple the Navier-Stokes equations with Maxwell's equations. Under the low magnetic Reynolds number approximation, the Lorentz force $\mathbf{F}_L = \mathbf{J} \times \mathbf{B}$ enters the momentum equation:

$$\frac{\partial \mathbf{u}}{\partial t} + (\mathbf{u} \cdot \nabla)\mathbf{u} = -\frac{1}{\rho}\nabla p + \nu\nabla^2\mathbf{u} + \mathbf{g}\beta(T - T_0) + \frac{1}{\rho}(\mathbf{J} \times \mathbf{B})$$

Here, $\mathbf{J}$ is the current density and $\mathbf{B}$ the magnetic field.

Key dimensionless numbers include:

- **Rayleigh number (Ra):** Measures the buoyancy-driven flow intensity.
- **Prandtl number (Pr):** Ratio of momentum diffusivity to thermal diffusivity.

- **Hartmann number (Ha):** Quantifies the influence of the magnetic field on the flow.
- **Magnetic Reynolds number (Rm):** Ratio of magnetic advection to diffusion.

3. Stability and Onset of Convection

Stability analysis examines when a quiescent fluid layer heated from below becomes unstable to convective motion. The critical Rayleigh number Rac determines this onset.

In the presence of a magnetic field, the critical conditions change depending on field strength and orientation. Magnetic fields tend to stabilize the fluid, increasing Rac.

4. Nonlinear Behavior and Flow Patterns

While linear stability analysis provides critical insight into the conditions for the onset of convection, real-world convective flows often evolve beyond this threshold into rich, nonlinear regimes characterized by complex spatiotemporal structures. The nonlinear interactions between velocity, temperature, and magnetic fields generate a variety of flow patterns including steady convection rolls, hexagonal cells, oscillatory convection, and even chaotic or turbulent states.

5. Applications

The study of hydrodynamic and magnetohydrodynamic (MHD) convective flows is critical to understanding a wide range of natural and engineered systems. The complex interplay between buoyancy forces and magnetic fields governs the behavior and efficiency of processes spanning geophysics, astrophysics, and engineering technologies.

Geophysical flows: One of the most significant natural applications of MHD convection is found in the Earth's outer core. The outer core consists predominantly of molten iron and nickel — electrically conducting fluids — undergoing vigorous thermal and compositional convection due to heat loss to the mantle and inner core growth. These convective motions, strongly influenced by Earth's rotation and magnetic fields, generate and sustain the planet's geomagnetic field through the dynamo effect.

- **Geomagnetic Field Generation:** The interaction between convective flows and magnetic fields in the Earth's core leads to self-excited dynamo action, which maintains the geomagnetic field that shields the planet from harmful solar radiation.

- **Core-Mantle Interactions:** Variations in convective patterns affect the secular variation of the geomagnetic field, linking fluid dynamics to geodynamo modeling and seismic observations.

Understanding MHD convection in the core helps interpret paleomagnetic records, predict magnetic reversals, and model geodynamical phenomena such as the formation of the South Atlantic Anomaly.

Astrophysical plasmas: MHD convection also plays a fundamental role in stellar interiors and astrophysical plasma environments:

- **Stellar Convection Zones:** In stars like the Sun, outer convection zones consist of ionized plasma where buoyancy-driven flows interact with magnetic fields, generating magnetic activity cycles (e.g., sunspots, solar flares) via dynamo mechanisms similar to Earth's core.
- **Magnetic Star Formation:** Convection influenced by magnetic fields affects the transport of angular momentum and energy in star-forming regions, influencing the initial mass function and stellar evolution.
- **Accretion Disks and Cosmic Jets:** MHD convective instabilities contribute to turbulence and magnetic field amplification in accretion disks around black holes and neutron stars, impacting jet formation and high-energy emissions.

Engineering: In industrial contexts, MHD convection is harnessed or mitigated to optimize thermal management and fluid control in electrically conducting fluids:

- **Liquid Metal Cooling Systems:** High-performance nuclear reactors and concentrated solar power plants use liquid metals (e.g., sodium, lead-bismuth eutectic) as coolants due to their superior thermal conductivity. Controlling MHD convection in these systems is vital for efficient heat transfer and safety, as magnetic fields induced by currents or external sources affect flow patterns and turbulence.
- **MHD Pumps and Flow Control:** Magnetohydrodynamic pumps exploit the Lorentz force to drive fluid motion without mechanical components, useful in corrosive or high-temperature environments where traditional pumps fail.

- **Crystal Growth and Material Processing:** MHD convection influences the uniformity and quality of crystal growth in semiconductor manufacturing, where precise thermal control and suppression of unwanted flow instabilities are critical.

6. Challenges and Future Directions

Open questions remain in turbulent MHD convection, multiphase flows, and nonlinear dynamics under complex magnetic field configurations. Advances in numerical simulations and laboratory experiments are key to progress.

References

1. Chandrasekhar, S. (1961). *Hydrodynamic and Hydromagnetic Stability.* Oxford University Press.
2. Davidson, P. A. (2016). *Introduction to Magnetohydrodynamics (2nd ed.).* Cambridge University Press.
3. Moffatt, H. K. (1978). *Magnetic Field Generation in Electrically Conducting Fluids. Cambridge University Press.*
4. Aurnou, J., Calkins, M. A., Cheng, J. S., Julien, K., King, E. M., Nieves, D., Soderlund, K. M., & Stellmach, S. (2015). *Rotating convective turbulence in Earth and planetary cores. Physics of the Earth and Planetary Interiors, 246,* 52–71. https://doi.org/10.1016/j.pepi.2015.03.005
5. Roberts, P. H., & Glatzmaier, G. A. (2000). *Geodynamo theory and simulations. Reviews of Modern Physics, 72(4),* 1081–1123. https://doi.org/10.1103/RevModPhys.72.1081
6. Busse, F. H. (2002). *Convective flows in rapidly rotating spheres and their dynamo action. Physics of Fluids, 14(4),* 1301–1314. https://doi.org/10.1063/1.1445457
7. Gilman, P. A. (1983). *Magnetohydrodynamic "shallow water" equations for the solar tachocline. The Astrophysical Journal Supplement Series, 53,* 243–274. https://doi.org/10.1086/190841
8. Knaepen, B., & Moreau, R. (2008). *Magnetohydrodynamic turbulence at low magnetic Reynolds number. Annual Review of Fluid Mechanics, 40, 25–45.* https://doi.org/10.1146/annurev.fluid.40.111406.102227
9. Moreau, R. (1990). *Magnetohydrodynamics. Kluwer Academic Publishers.*
10. Zel'dovich, Y. B., Ruzmaikin, A. A., & Sokoloff, D. D. (1990). *The Almighty Chance. World Scientific.*

11. *Molokov, S., Moreau, R., & Moffatt, H. K. (Eds.). (2007). Magnetohydrodynamics: Historical Evolution and Trends. Springer.*
12. *Lappa, M. (2010). Thermal Convection: Patterns, Evolution and Stability. Wiley-VCH.*
13. *Thess, A., & Zikanov, O. (2007). Suppression of turbulence in magnetohydrodynamic flows. Physics of Fluids, 19(7), 074104. https://doi.org/10.1063/1.2759655*
14. *Aurnou, J. M., Andreadis, S., Zhu, L., & Olson, P. (2003). Experiments on convection in Earth's core tangent cylinder. Geophysical Journal International, 152(3), 729–740. https://doi.org/10.1046/j.1365-246X.2003.01811.x*
15. *Shercliff, J. A. (1965). A Textbook of Magnetohydrodynamics. Pergamon Press.*

CHAPTER TWENTY-TWO

Empowering Women, Transforming Economics

Author: *Manish Kumar Tiwari (Research Scholar, Sam Higginbottom University of Agriculture Technology & Sciences), Prayagraj*
Co-Author: *Dr.Enid Masih (Associate Professor, Sam Higginbottom University of Agriculture Technology & Sciences), Prayagraj*

Abstract

Women's empowerment is a fundamental driver of sustainable economic transformation worldwide. By expanding women's access to education, finance, leadership, and entrepreneurial opportunities, societies unlock new sources of innovation, productivity, and inclusive growth. This chapter explores the multifaceted relationship between women's empowerment and economic change, emphasizing how gender equity advances development goals, reshapes labor markets, and enhances societal well-being. Strategies and policies that enable women to overcome structural barriers and actively participate in economic decision-making are examined alongside global case studies demonstrating transformative impact.

Keywords: Women's empowerment, economic transformation, gender equity, inclusive growth, entrepreneurship, education, financial inclusion, leadership.

1. Introduction

Empowering women is not only a matter of social justice but a critical economic imperative. Globally, increased female labor force participation, entrepreneurship, and leadership contribute significantly to economic productivity and poverty reduction. Empowered women drive innovation, improve household welfare, and foster more resilient economies. However, despite progress, gender disparities persist in education, employment, and access to resources, limiting the full potential of women as economic agents of change.

This chapter examines the pathways through which empowering women catalyzes economic transformation. It highlights the interplay between gender equity and economic structures and presents evidence-based strategies for harnessing women's capabilities to build inclusive and sustainable economies.

2. The Economic Case for Women's Empowerment

Extensive empirical research and economic analysis consistently demonstrate that gender equality and women's empowerment are not just social goals but essential drivers of sustained economic growth and development. When women are empowered to participate fully in economic activities, the benefits extend beyond individual gains to national and global economies, reshaping labor markets, innovation capacity, and social welfare.

Increasing Labor Supply and Diversifying Talent Pools

Women constitute roughly half of the global population, yet in many countries, their labor force participation remains significantly lower than men's. Empowering women to enter and remain in the workforce expands the overall labor supply, which is crucial for economies facing aging populations and labor shortages. Moreover, diversity in the workforce brings varied perspectives, experiences, and skills, which foster creativity and problem-solving—key components for economic dynamism and competitiveness.

Enhancing Productivity Through Improved Skills and Innovation

Women's empowerment often involves access to education and skill development, which directly enhances productivity. Educated women contribute not only as workers but as innovators and entrepreneurs, driving technological adoption and business model innovation. Studies have found that gender-diverse teams tend to perform better and create more innovative products, thereby boosting firm-level productivity and economic output.

Strengthening Human Capital by Investing in Children's Health and Education

Research shows that women tend to invest a larger proportion of their income into their children's health, nutrition, and education compared to men. This investment leads to the development of a healthier, more educated future workforce, creating a virtuous cycle that improves economic prospects over generations. Empowering women economically thus has multiplier effects, influencing human capital accumulation and long-term growth.

Expanding Entrepreneurship, Driving Job Creation and Market Dynamism

Women entrepreneurs contribute significantly to job creation and economic diversification. By fostering women-led businesses, economies benefit from increased competition, innovation, and inclusive growth. Empowering women in entrepreneurship often unlocks untapped markets and stimulates local economies, especially in sectors such as agriculture, retail, and services where women predominate.

Promoting More Equitable Income Distribution and Social Cohesion

Gender equality contributes to reducing income disparities and poverty. Empowered women's earnings help narrow household income gaps and improve living standards. This equitable distribution promotes social cohesion and stability, which are essential for sustained economic development. Economies with higher gender parity also tend to have better governance, lower corruption, and stronger institutional frameworks.

Economic Impact in Numbers

According to the McKinsey Global Institute (2015), closing gender gaps in labor force participation, education, and entrepreneurial activity could add as much as $12 trillion—equivalent to the size of the entire U.S. and China economies combined—to global GDP by 2025. Furthermore, countries that actively promote women's empowerment demonstrate greater economic resilience during downturns, as a more inclusive labor market and diversified economic base help absorb shocks and accelerate recovery.

In summary, empowering women catalyzes a broad spectrum of economic benefits, making gender equality an essential strategy not only for social justice but also for achieving robust and sustainable economic transformation.

3. Key Dimensions of Women's Empowerment Transforming Economics

3.1 Education and Skill Development

Education is a cornerstone of women's empowerment and a critical enabler of economic transformation. Access to quality education and vocational training equips women with the knowledge and skills necessary to participate fully in the workforce, pursue entrepreneurship, and contribute to innovation. For women, especially in developing economies, education opens doors to higher-value employment opportunities and positions them to compete in fast-growing and technologically advanced sectors.

- **Quality Education: Building Foundations for Economic Participation** Ensuring that girls and women have access to foundational education—literacy, numeracy, and critical thinking—is essential. Higher levels of education correlate with better employment prospects, higher earnings, and improved health and social outcomes. Unfortunately, many regions still face challenges such as gender gaps in school enrollment, early dropouts, and inadequate educational infrastructure, limiting women's economic potential.
- **Vocational Training and Lifelong Learning** Beyond formal schooling, vocational training and continuous skill development programs offer women pathways into skilled trades and emerging industries. These programs are particularly effective in bridging the gap between education and employment, especially for marginalized women who may lack traditional academic credentials.
- **Emphasizing STEM and Digital Skills** The rapid advancement of technology and the rise of the digital economy make STEM (Science, Technology, Engineering, and Mathematics) education and digital literacy critical for future economic opportunities. Women remain underrepresented in STEM fields globally, which constrains their participation in high-growth sectors such as information technology, engineering, data science, and biotechnology. Efforts to promote STEM education among girls and women help address these disparities. This includes early engagement in science and math subjects, scholarships for women in STEM higher education, and targeted programs that dismantle stereotypes and gender biases in these fields.
- **Bridging the Digital Divide** Digital skills are increasingly vital not only for formal employment but also for entrepreneurship and access to online markets. Training women in digital literacy, coding, and the use of emerging technologies empowers them to leverage digital platforms for economic activities, from e-commerce to remote work and freelancing.
- **Economic and Social Impact** Countries that invest in women's education and skills development reap substantial economic returns, including higher productivity, innovation capacity, and social well-being. Empowered through education, women tend to have greater control over

their economic choices and are more likely to advocate for community development and gender equality.

3.2 Financial Inclusion

Financial inclusion is a fundamental pillar in empowering women economically, providing them with the tools and resources to build assets, start or expand businesses, and manage financial risks. Access to formal financial services—such as credit, savings, insurance, and payment systems—enables women to increase their economic independence and resilience. Yet, women worldwide often face significant barriers in accessing these services, perpetuating economic disparities.

- **Access to Credit: Fueling Women's Entrepreneurship** Credit access is critical for women entrepreneurs to start or scale businesses. However, many women face difficulties due to lack of collateral, limited credit histories, and gender bias within financial institutions. These constraints restrict their ability to invest in productive assets, inventory, technology, and workforce expansion. Tailored credit products designed with women's needs in mind—such as lower collateral requirements and flexible repayment schedules—can significantly improve access.
- **Encouraging Savings and Asset Building** Savings services empower women to build financial cushions for emergencies and future investments. Group savings models, such as Self-Help Groups (SHGs) and rotating savings and credit associations (ROSCAs), have proven effective in many communities by leveraging social capital and peer support. Encouraging savings habits enhances women's bargaining power within households and communities.
- **Insurance and Risk Mitigation** Insurance products tailored for women, including health, life, and crop insurance for rural entrepreneurs, help mitigate economic vulnerabilities. Protection against unforeseen risks reduces the likelihood that women must sell productive assets or withdraw children from school during financial crises.
- **The Role of Fintech and Digital Finance** Innovations in financial technology (fintech) are transforming the landscape of financial inclusion for women. Mobile banking, digital wallets, and online lending platforms reduce physical and social barriers to accessing financial services. These digital tools are especially important in rural or underserved areas where traditional banking infrastructure is limited.

Fintech solutions also provide alternative credit scoring using non-traditional data, enabling women without formal credit histories to obtain loans. Moreover, digital platforms facilitate women's participation in the digital economy, from online businesses to gig work.

- **Addressing the Gender Finance Gap** Despite progress, the gender finance gap remains substantial. Women are 20-30% less likely than men to have access to formal financial services, and this gap is wider in low-income countries. Bridging this divide requires gender-responsive policies, financial literacy programs tailored for women, and partnerships between governments, financial institutions, and civil society to develop inclusive financial ecosystems.

- **Economic Impact** Improved financial inclusion for women has wide-reaching economic benefits. It promotes entrepreneurship, job creation, and household welfare. Studies indicate that women's financial empowerment leads to increased investment in children's health and education, accelerating intergenerational economic mobility.

3.3 Entrepreneurship and Business Leadership

Supporting women-owned businesses is pivotal for fostering innovation and driving economic diversification. Targeted programs that provide access to mentorship, business development services, and financing enable women entrepreneurs to scale their ventures and compete effectively in the marketplace. Furthermore, facilitating market access—through supplier diversity initiatives, networking opportunities, and digital platforms—helps women-led enterprises expand their customer base and integrate into broader value chains. These efforts not only empower individual entrepreneurs but also stimulate job creation and contribute to resilient, inclusive economies. Governments, private sector actors, and civil society must collaborate to dismantle structural barriers and cultivate ecosystems that nurture women's entrepreneurial leadership.

3.4 Labor Market Participation and Equal Opportunity

Ensuring women's full participation in the labor market requires robust policies that address structural inequalities and promote fair treatment. Equal pay legislation helps close persistent wage gaps, while comprehensive maternity and parental benefits support women's continued engagement in the workforce. Workplace safety regulations and anti-discrimination laws create environments where women feel secure and valued. Together, these measures not only enhance women's economic empowerment but also improve organizational productivity and social equity. By fostering inclusive labor markets, policymakers and employers enable women to contribute meaningfully to—and benefit equitably from—sustained economic growth.

3.5 Political and Economic Decision-Making

Women's representation in governance structures, corporate boards, and policymaking bodies is essential for shaping inclusive economic agendas that reflect diverse perspectives and needs. Increased participation of women in decision-making roles enhances transparency, accountability, and responsiveness to social equity concerns. Research shows that gender-diverse leadership contributes to more balanced policy outcomes and corporate strategies, fostering sustainable economic development. Encouraging women's involvement at these levels requires targeted measures such as gender quotas, leadership training, and supportive networks, which help dismantle systemic barriers and empower women to influence economic priorities and governance reforms effectively.

4. Overcoming Barriers to Empowerment

Despite the clear economic and social benefits of women's empowerment, persistent barriers continue to hinder progress. Deeply entrenched cultural norms often restrict women's mobility, limit their ambitions, and confine them to traditional roles centered around unpaid care work. These unequal care responsibilities reduce time and energy available for education, employment, and entrepreneurship. Additionally, gender-based violence and workplace harassment undermine women's safety, confidence, and ability to participate fully in economic life. Compounding these challenges are legal and policy gaps, particularly in areas such as property ownership and inheritance rights, which curtail women's economic agency and access to resources. Addressing these multifaceted barriers requires integrated approaches that combine social change initiatives, legal reforms, and economic policies. Community-level awareness campaigns and advocacy play a vital role in transforming societal attitudes and ensuring that reforms translate into tangible empowerment outcomes.

5. Policy and Programmatic Strategies

Effective empowerment of women requires comprehensive policies and programs designed with a gender-responsive lens. Gender-responsive budgeting ensures that public resources are allocated to address women's specific needs and priorities, fostering equitable development outcomes.

Investing in girls' education and lifelong learning equips women with the skills necessary to compete in evolving labor markets, especially in STEM and digital sectors. Financial literacy programs combined with gender-sensitive credit schemes improve women's access to capital and enable informed financial decision-making. Support networks, mentorship programs, and leadership development initiatives provide critical social capital and capacity-building opportunities, helping women overcome barriers and advance in their careers and businesses. Additionally, strengthening legal protections—through anti-discrimination laws, enforcement mechanisms, and awareness campaigns—ensures that women's rights are upheld in workplaces and communities, creating safer and more equitable environments for economic participation.

6. Case Studies: Women Empowering Economies

Several countries offer compelling examples of how empowering women catalyzes economic transformation. In Rwanda, comprehensive post-genocide gender reforms significantly increased women's political representation and fostered entrepreneurship, playing a crucial role in the nation's rapid economic recovery and social rebuilding. Bangladesh demonstrates the power of microfinance and Self-Help Group (SHG) models, which have lifted millions of women out of poverty by promoting financial inclusion, entrepreneurship, and community solidarity. The Nordic countries provide a model of how comprehensive welfare systems and proactive gender equality policies create enabling environments for women's labor force participation, contributing to some of the world's most robust and resilient economies. In India's tech sector, women-led startups are reshaping innovation landscapes, driving job creation, and challenging traditional gender norms within a rapidly growing industry. These case studies underscore the diverse pathways and strategies through which women's empowerment fosters inclusive and sustainable economic growth.

7. Conclusion

Empowering women is a transformative lever for economic change. By investing in women's education, financial access, entrepreneurship, and leadership, societies can unlock inclusive growth and sustainable development. Addressing persistent barriers and fostering enabling environments is critical to ensuring that women not only participate in but also lead economic transformation.

References

1. McKinsey Global Institute. (2015). *The Power of Parity: How Advancing Women's Equality Can Add $12 Trillion to Global Growth.*

2. Kabeer, N. (2016). *Women's Economic Empowerment and Inclusive Growth: Labour Markets and Enterprise Development. International Development Research Centre.*

3. World Bank. (2019). *Women, Business and the Law 2019: A Decade of Reform.*

4. UN Women. (2020). *The Economic Empowerment of Women: An Overview.*

5. Duflo, E. (2012). *Women Empowerment and Economic Development. Journal of Economic Literature, 50(4), 1051–1079.*

6. OECD. (2017). *The Pursuit of Gender Equality: An Uphill Battle.*

7. Sen, A. (1999). *Development as Freedom. Oxford University Press.*